Four Two-Act Plays

Other Plays by Sam Shepard

Action
Angel City
Back Bog Beast Bait
Buried Child
Chicago
Cowboy Mouth
Cowboys # 2
Curse of the Starving Class
Forensic and the Navigator
Fourteen Hundred Thousand
The Holy Ghostly
Icarus's Mother
Killer's Head
The Mad Dog Blues
Melodrama Play
Red Cross
Seduced
Shaved Splits
Suicide in B^b
The Rock Garden
The Unseen Hand
Up to Thursday
4-H Club

Four Two-Act Plays

by

Sam Shepard

Urizen Books • New York

La Turista © 1968 by Sam Shepard
The Tooth of Crime © 1974 by Sam Shepard
Geography of a Horse Dreamer © 1974 by Sam Shepard
Operation Sidewinder © 1970 by Sam Shepard

All inquiries concerning performing rights should be addressed to the author's agent, Toby Cole, c/o Samuel French, Inc., 25 West 45th Street, New York, NY 10036.

Printed in the United States of America

ISBN 0-89396-020-9 (cloth)
 0-89396-021-7 (paper)

Library of Congress Catalog Card Number 80-53868

Library of Congress Cataloging in Publication Data

Shepard, Sam, 1943 —
 Four two-act plays.

 CONTENTS: La turista.—The tooth of crime.—
Geography of a horse dreamer.—Operation sidewinder.
 I. Title.
PS3569.H394F6   812'.54

© 1980 by Sam Shepard

Contents

La Turista

For
JOYCE

La Turista opened at The American Place Theatre in New York City on 4th March 1967, for a limited engagement of two weeks. It was directed by Jacques Levy, and the cast for the original production were as follows:

SALEM	Joyce Aaron
KENT	Sam Waterston
BOY	Lawrence Block
DOCTOR	Michael Lombard
SON	Joel Novack
DOC	Michael Lombard
SONNY	Lawrence Block

The London production opened at the Theatre Upstairs of the Royal Court Theatre on 18th March 1969 with the following cast:

SALEM	Lelia Goldoni
KENT	Barry Dennen
BOY	Al Mancini
DOCTOR	George Margo
SON	Chris Cabot
DOC	George Margo
SONNY	Al Mancini

Directed by Roger Hendricks-Simon

INTRODUCTION

A few lines, as a prologue to my review of Sam Shepard's *La Turista* which is reprinted here just as it was written immediately after seeing the play. I have, in the months since, thought again and again about this play and the imaginative strength of it. From the moment I entered the American Place Theatre I was caught up in the violent energy of a new work. It is hard to forget the bright, bright yellow and orange set, so hard and brilliant, so open, glaring and aggressive, that announced the bright, glaring, aggressive brilliance of the play.

Some further thoughts about the text occur to me. Nothing is harder to come by than a truly meaningful central image, one that opens out to possibility, encourages invention. For some reason we must, aesthetically, be satisfied with the image, or situation, on the first plane of concreteness. Without that it is hard to give assent to the elaborations that will follow; in a sense, you have to enter the structure the author gives you before you are willing to see what is inside. In this play the identity of the person—the tourist—and his affliction, that humbling diarrhoea—"la turista"—are signified by a single word. This word and the two things it represents are the bare centre of the play, the ruling image. The sickness is a sort of a joke—that kills.

Salem and Kent are literally tourists in Mexico in the first act. In the second, which in point of time takes place before the first, Kent is on another kind of journey—I won't say "trip"—in which American rhetoric is offered for his cure just as the blood of freshly killed chickens had been offered in "primitive" Mexico. Neither works.

Perhaps the characters are not profitably thought of as characters at all. They are actors, parodists. They slip from style to style; they carry a few props around with them as they change their roles; they "freeze" when they want to withdraw from the action on the stage. The essence of their being is energy, verbal energy. In the restless inventiveness of their parodies and tirades, a storm of feeling and experience blows across the stage. The parts are arias. In the last section of Act Two Doc and Kent "sing" an extraordinary duet. These arias have to do with death. It is amazing the number of "deaths" that will fit the text: Vietnam, Santo Domingo, racial violence, drop-outs, colonialism.

When I wrote about the play, I gave more attention to the critics than I think it is worth now. And yet that was a part of the scenery in which the first production of the play took place. I would have felt very sorry if I had missed seeing it and I must confess that I hated to see it close. But this play lives on the page, and that is a rare thing nowadays.

September 1967

*　　*　　*　　*　　*

March 1967

La Turista by Sam Shepard, in a dazzling production at the American Place Theatre, is a work of superlative interest. The reviewers have not been invited to submit an evaluation of the play. It is merely there, for a month, appearing for the membership of the American Place and for those who find their way to it. I have no knowledge of the intentions and feelings about the reviewers or those responsible for this play; I went to it of my own free will and write about it under no duress and without asking permission. Still, it appears logical that when a play invites the press it is making a sort of plea or demand that the reviewer, under his contractual obligations to his publication, offer some comment about what he has seen. He may not have wished to go and he may not wish to write; he is a captive, arbitrarily condemned to the formation of an opinion. The production, by its foolhardy solicitations, condemns itself to the recognition of the opinions. Play and critic, thereby, become linked like suspect and detective.

The night I saw *La Turista* the American Place audience was, for the most part, utterly depressing; middle-aged, middle class, and rather aggressively indifferent: a dead weight of alligators, dozing and grunting before muddily sliding away. It felt like nothing so much as those same old evenings in our theatre, evenings with the reviewers spaced about like stop signs. A further step in the liberation of the theatre became evident: not only must the reviewers be freed of their obligation to go to a play, but the audience they have created, their bent twigs, should not be the object of special encouragement. It is hard to imagine anyone acting under the influence of the inchoate homilies of, for instance, Richard Watts who looks after our local and national morals for us, but, even in the case of *La Turista*, one could *imagine* a line slowly forming outside some box office and the people whispering, "Walter Kerr sort of liked it a little, and you know *he* never likes anything." But, indeed, what good does it do a man to go to see something he won't like just because the reviewers have told him to do so? He would be better off at home. Our new American theatre cannot play to the old audience; it must have a new one.

In *La Turista* there is the piognant meeting on some pure level of understanding of playwright, director, and actor: the sort of unity that makes the Royal Shakespeare's production of *The Homecoming* so rare. Jacques Levy, the director, is a theatrical talent of unremitting inspiration. The actors are all first-rate, but in Sam Waterston the play has a young actor of such versatility and charm that one hardly knows how to express the degree of his talents. With this play, the promise of the lofts of off-off Broadway, the dedication and independence, come to the most extraordinary fulfilment. You do not feel you are being given a package, assembled for a purpose, and in some way this is disconcerting to the senses. The audience, accustomed to ensembles created as a calculation, may feel left out, slow to respond, trapped by a sluggish metabolism. In the long run, what is so beautiful is the graceful—in spite of the frenzied energy—concentration of the work as a whole, and for that, if one would take it in, the audience also has to work.

Sam Shepard, the author of *La Turista*, is twenty-three years old and even so he is not new to the theatre. He is not being "discovered" in this production. His plays have been off-off, in the Café La Mama repertory; he has been at the Cherry Lane and will soon be in print. *La Turista* is his most ambitious play thus far but still it is in the same style and voice as *Chicago* and his other one-act plays. The scene opens on an electrifying set: a bright, bright formica yellow hotel room in Mexico. A young American couple—Salem and Kent—are sitting up in their twin beds. They are covered with a deep bronze suntan make-up and are holding their arms out stiffly. On the beach, as a part of their vacation, they have gotten a painful sunburn. They talk of first, second, and third—and *fourth* degree burns.

"Well, the epidermis is actually cooked, fried like a piece of meat over a charcoal fire. The molecular structure of the fatty tissue is partially destroyed by the sun rays, and so the blood rushes to the surface to repair the damage."
". . . it's just the blood rushing to the surface."

Mock scientific dialogue, inserted merely for itself, delivered in a cool, matter-of-fact way, but sharply, insistently, is characteristic of the writing. (Of course, the couple with their expensive, painful sunburns will bring to mind those other burns of our time.) The players hardly ever look at each other. There is a feeling of declamation, rather than of conversation or dialogue. And yet the monologues do not at all suggest that banality of Broadway—the "failure of communication"—but actually are quite the opposite. They are an extreme of communication. Kent, the young man, also has, in addition to his sunburn, "la turista", the intestinal distress that affects Americans when they visit poor countries like Mexico. At this point in the play, a young Mexican enters. He is one of the world's poor, with his American phrases ("I had to follow this cat around with a palm fan while he scored on all the native chicks.")—he begs and yet he is intractable, unmanageable. He spits in the young American's face.

As the act progresses, Kent becomes very ill. Two wonderfully absurd witch-doctors, Mexican style, are brought in, with

live roosters, candles, voodoo and crucifixes. Kent dies, a
sacrifice to "la turista"—his lack of resistance to the germs of
the country he arrogantly patronizes with his presence. The
second act has all the same elements as the first, but they are
acted out in a Summit Hotel sort of room in America and the
witch-doctors are two circuit rider charlatans in Civil War
dress. Here Kent dies of sleeping sickness, or perhaps he is
on drugs; in any case he has an American disease this time—
he doesn't like to be awake. His final monologue is a psychedelic tirade—and he jumps, in his pajamas, through the hotel
wall, leaving the print of the outlines of his body in the wall-
paper.

George Eliot said that she wrote her novels out of the belief
in "the orderly sequence by which the seed brings forth a
crop of its kind." We all have a nostalgia and longing for this
order because it has been the heart of European fiction and
drama. Incident after incident, each growing out of the other,
united in a chain of significant motivation, of cause and effect
—moments of human destiny strung out like beads on a string.
This is what we mean, perhaps, when we say we "understand"
a work of literary art. Yet each decade brings us the conviction
that this order is no longer present to the serious writer. It
is most appealing to those writers who construct their works
for some possibility of the market-place. The episodic, the
obscurely related, the collection of images, moods: connec-
tions in fiction and also in drama have become like those of
poetry. Tone and style hold the work together, create whatever emotional effect it will have upon us. Out of episodes and
images, characters and conflicts are made, but they are of a
blurred and complex sort.

Formless images and meaningless happenings are peculiarly
oppressive to the spirit, and the inanities of the experimental
theatre could make a man commit suicide. Sam Shepard, on
the other hand, possesses the most impressive literary talent
and dramatic inventiveness. He is voluble, in love with long,
passionate, intense monologues (both of the acts end in these
spasms of speech) which almost petrify the audience. His play
ends with sweating, breathless actors in a state of exhaustion.

The characters put on a shawl and begin to declaim like an auctioneer at a slave mart, or a cowboy suit and fall into Texas harangues. They stop in the midst of jokes, for set pieces, some fixed action from childhood, perhaps influenced by the bit in Albee's *Zoo Story*. Despair and humour, each of a peculiarly expressive kind, are the elements out of which the script of the play is made. The effect is very powerful and if it cannot be reduced to one or two themes it is still clearly about us and our lives. The diction, the action, the direction, the ideas are completely American and it is our despair and humour Shepard gets on to the stage.

To return to the decision about the critics: it is a sacrificial act of the most serious sort. It means nothing less than, after a fixed short run, if one is lucky enough to have that, the play may suffer simple cessation for want of those and good and bad advertisements combed from the newspapers and television. Perhaps it is only young people, free of deforming ambitions, who would have the courage to submit to such a test. Or perhaps it is the strength of their art that allows them to wait for what will come or not come. There are worse things than silence.

ELIZABETH HARDWICK

ACT ONE

SCENE. *Two single beds with clean white sheets and pillows upstage centre. Between the beds is a small yellow desk with a telephone on it. The entire upstage wall is bright canary yellow. A bright orange door in the wall to stage right with the words "CUARTO DE BANO" printed on it in red letters. Another bright orange door, stage left, with a cardboard sign hanging by string from the doorknob. The sign reads "NO MOLESTAR POR FAVOR" in red letters. At the foot of each bed, on the floor, are two huge over-stuffed suitcases. A large fan hangs from the ceiling, centre stage. SALEM, a woman in panties and bra, sits on the stage left bed propped up with a pillow, facing the audience and reading Life magazine. KENT, a man in underwear, sits in the same position on the stage right bed reading Time magazine. Both SALEM and KENT have bright red skin. The lights come up to bright yellow, the fan is on, SALEM and KENT sit reading for a while. They continue reading as they talk.*

SALEM: The woman in—where was it? Puerto Juarez or something. The very rich Spanish woman. Remember? The young woman with her mother who spoke such good English. Very rich.

KENT: What did she say?

SALEM: She said the white of an egg is what you use for second or third degree burns. The pain is eased right away. What happens when the skin is burned? I mean what actually happens?

KENT: Well, the epidermis is actually cooked, fried like a piece of meat over a charcoal fire. The molecular structure of the fatty tissue is partially destroyed by the sun rays, and so the blood rushes to the surface to repair the damage.

SALEM: So your skin doesn't really turn red like magic, it's just the blood rushing to the surface.

KENT: Right.

SALEM: So Mexicans aren't really tan, are they. They just have darker skin, tougher skin with a tighter fatty molecular structure.

KENT: I think that's an anthropological argument now, where some say the dark-skinned people of the earth were born that way to begin with for camouflage reasons to protect them against death, and others say it was to protect them against the sun.

SALEM: It doesn't make much difference.

KENT: No. But the sun theory seems to make more sense. Well no, I guess the death theory makes more sense since Icelandic people, people who live in snowy places, have light skin to match the snow. So I guess it has to do with camouflage, since camouflage has to do with deceiving death.

SALEM: What about Eskimos.

KENT: Eskimos are more on the yellow side, aren't they. More Mongoloid. Eskimos aren't really dark.

SALEM: Well, Mexicans are more Mongoloid than Negroid and you call them dark.

KENT: That's true. (KENT *jumps to his feet and starts for the stage door right and then stops short.*)

SALEM: Que paso!

KENT: I started to feel it coming and then it stopped. I don't know whether it's coming or stopping.

SALEM: Que turista! No!

KENT: Speak English, will you. (*He starts again for the door and stops.*)

SALEM: Is it dysentery?

KENT: I don't know. It starts and stops.

SALEM (*like a nurse*): Cramps in the stomach?

KENT: Slight ones.

SALEM: Nausea?

KENT: Slight.

SALEM: Rumbling in the bowels?

KENT: A little.

SALEM: Esta turista?

(KENT *starts to run for the door and stops again.*)

KENT: You sound glad or something.

SALEM: No. Yo es muy simpatico.

KENT: We both ate the same food, you know, so you'll be getting it soon too.

SALEM: My metabolism is very high.

(KENT *returns to the stage right bed, picks up the magazine, and continues to read.*)

KENT: Relaxation is the thing you seek. You spend thousands of hours and dollars and plane rides to get to a place for relaxation. To just disappear for a while. And you wind up like this. With diarrhoea.

SALEM: You came here to disappear?

KENT: That's right. Didn't you? To relax and disappear.

SALEM: What would you do if you did disappear?

KENT: Nothing. I'd be gone.

SALEM: I ask you that face to face. It deserves to be answered.

KENT: Do you know how soon it is before you can start peeling it?

SALEM: Not before it's dead, I can tell you that much. Right now it stings. That means it's alive and hurting. Pretty soon it itches. Then you know it's dying. Then it stops itching and you know it's dead. Then you can start peeling. Not before.

KENT: You can start peeling as soon as it begins to itch. I know that much. That's when you itch so you scratch it and that gets you peeling.

SALEM: You can't start before the itching stops.

KENT: Why not? You could even start while it's still stinging if you wanted. You could even start before it starts stinging and get a head start.

SALEM: And then really get burned. You'd be in sad shape then, boy.

KENT: Then you start peeling again.

SALEM: There's only three layers, you know. It doesn't go on for ever.

KENT: Obviously you've never heard of the fourth degree burn. A fourth degree burn is unheard of because it's never happened, but one day it will, and doctors will be dismayed from coast to coast, and a new word will be born into their language. *The Fourth Degree Burn!*

SALEM: What is it like! What is it like!

(KENT *rises on his bed and demonstrates for her.*)

KENT: The fourth degree burn comes about after the most extreme and excruciating process has taken its course. The first degree has already occurred and a layer has dropped away almost of its own accord. Effortlessly it floats to the floor at your feet and piles around your ankles like sheets of Kleenex. The second degree comes with a little more shock and a little more pain. It scrapes off like dust and covers the sheets.

SALEM: And now for the third!

KENT: Yes! But the third takes time. The third begins slowly and creeps along the surface, grabbing hold and easing up. Biting down and relaxing away until the spaces get fewer and the biting gets harder. Everything burns and everything you touch is as hot as the sun. You stand away from everything else. You stand in mid-air with space all around you. The ground is on fire. The breeze feels like boiling-hot water. The moon is just like the sun. You become a flame and dance in mid-air. The bottom is blue. The middle is yellow and changes to green. The top is red and changes to orange. The breeze dances with you. The flame reaches up and then shrinks and bursts into sparks. The ground bursts into flame and circles the breeze. The sparks dart through the breeze and dash back and forth hitting up against the flames, and——

(*The stage left door opens, and a dark-skinned boy, but not Negro, enters with bare feet and carrying a shoe shine kit. Both* SALEM *and* KENT *scream and pull the top sheet of their beds over their bodies so just their heads are sticking out. The boy crosses in between the beds and just stares at them with his hand out.*)

Basta!

SALEM: Vaya!

KENT: Give him some money.

SALEM: How do you say go away?

KENT: Just give him some money.

SALEM: I can't, it's in the suitcase.

KENT: Well get it.

SALEM: How do I get it?

KENT: Crawl down under the sheet and get it.

SALEM: Can't you get up?

KENT: Salem, you're the closest one to the money.

SALEM: Oh, all right.

(*She crawls underneath the sheet to the foot of the bed and sticks her hand out to reach the suitcase on the floor. As she does this,* KENT *speaks to the* BOY, *who just stares with his hand out.*)

KENT: She'll have it for you in just a second.

BOY: Lustre?

KENT: She'll be right with you. If you weren't so poor, I'd kick you out on your ass.

BOY: Lustre?

KENT: Just hold on. Are they taught by their mothers and fathers to look more despondent than they really are?
(SALEM *is still under the sheet and struggling to open the suitcase.*)

SALEM: Sometimes.

KENT: It works. All they have to do is stare. A blank stare does more than a grimace.

SALEM: Just stare back.

KENT: If I was that poor I'd kill myself. I wouldn't pretend I was sadder than I really was. I couldn't take it all the time, everywhere I went, every time I got up, knowing I was no better off and no worse than yesterday. Just the same all the time. Just poor.

BOY: Lustre?

KENT: To just go on and on, getting older and older, and staying just as poor, and maybe even getting poorer. And pretending all the time I was poorer than I was.

SALEM: That's why the mothers sometimes give their babies away to tourists, because they know there's a better chance of them getting rich.

KENT: Who'd want a poor kid?

SALEM: Some people who can't have a rich one.

BOY: Lustre?

KENT: What's he want?

SALEM: To shine your shoes.

KENT: No shine. Go away. Basta!

BOY: Lustre?

KENT: No! (*He puts his head under the sheet. The* BOY *just stands.*)

SALEM: Let him shine your shoes.

KENT: No! I can't even look at him. His hands are full of pork grease; his eyes are red; his breath smells. Get him away.

SALEM: Ah ha!

(*She opens the suitcase, and money pours out of it. She gestures with her hand for the* BOY *to come and take some money. Her hand is the only visible part of her.*)

SALEM: Aqui niño! Aqui!

(*The* BOY *keeps staring at* KENT, *who remains under the sheet.*)

KENT: Is he gone?

SALEM: Chico. Aqui. Quiere diñero? Por favor. Aqui.

KENT: What's he doing?

SALEM: Will you be quiet. He won't even move. He doesn't even know there's free money to be had.

KENT: Great.

SALEM: Niño por favor. Aqui. Es muy bueno.

(*This speech should sound like an English safari hunter warning somebody about a man-eating lion. During this,* SALEM'*s hand can be seen waving money at the* BOY. KENT *stays under the sheet through the speech.*)

KENT: He'll never leave now. He's probably never seen a house like this in his life. He grew up in a village, in a hut. He nursed his mother's milk until he was four and a half and then almost died from dysentery at the time he was weaned. He's eaten nothing but rice and beans all his life and slept on the dirt and sold dirty Coca Cola to passing cars. He'll never leave now no matter how much you give him. The fan to him is like the finest air conditioning. The beds to him are like two Rolls Royces. He likes the sound of my voice because it's so strange and soothing and he knows I'm talking about him, and he likes that because, where he lives in the jungle, nobody talks about him, because he's nothing different to them. They're all the same and silent, and sleep and walk around each other like herds of wild boar getting ready to run or kill each other, depending upon the air and the wind and the sun.

SALEM: Well what shall we do about that.

KENT: Can you reach the phone?

SALEM: You're closer to it than me.

KENT: O.K. Maybe the manager will know what to do.
(KENT *starts to reach for the phone. The* BOY *rushes to the phone and pulls it out of the wall, then crosses downstage centre with it and sets it on the floor. He sits down next to the phone and sets the shoe shine kit down and smiles at the audience. Throughout the following, the* BOY *makes different monster faces at the audience, from sticking his tongue out to giving them the finger.*)

SALEM (*still under the sheet*): What happened?

KENT (*now visible*): The little prick pulled the phone out of the wall. (SALEM *laughs.*) All right!
(KENT *jumps out of bed and crosses down to the* BOY, *who just sits centre stage facing the audience.*)

SALEM (*still under the sheets*): Are you out of bed, dear?

KENT (*to the* BOY): You have to leave now. This is not your home. Go back from where you come from.
(*The* BOY *stands and spits in* KENT's *face.* KENT *rushes back to the bed and wipes the spit off with the sheet. The* BOY *sits again and continues making faces to the audience.*)

KENT: OOOoooh! Oh my God! Aaaah! Spit! He spit on me! Oh no! Oh my God! Jesus! He spit on me!

SALEM: What's the matter?

KENT: He spit! He spit! He spit all over me. Oh my God!
(*He wipes himself frantically with the sheet. The* BOY *smiles at the audience.* SALEM *works her way under the sheets to the head of the bed and pokes her head out.*)

SALEM: What's going on?

KENT: Oh, I can't stand it. The little prick! Oh God! I'll have to take a shower! Aaah! Oh my God! What a rotten thing to do!

(*He rushes to the stage right door and goes inside, slamming
the door behind him.* SALEM *speaks to the* BOY *from the bed.
The* BOY *does not turn to her but continues making faces to
the audience.* KENT *can be heard groaning behind the door.*)

SALEM : When I was about ten I think, little boy, I'd just returned
home from a car trip to the county fair with my family. My
father, my mother, my sisters and brothers. We'd just gotten
home after driving for about two hours, and it had just
gotten dark, but none of us had spoken for the whole trip.
Are you listening. It was the same as though we'd all been
asleep, and we drove in the driveway, and my father stopped
the car. But instead of any of us getting out right away like
we usually did we all just sat in the car staring ahead and
not speaking for a very long time. I was the first to get out
and start walking toward the cement steps that led to the
porch and I could hear my family behind me. My father,
my mother, my sisters and brothers. And I could hear all
four doors of the car slam one after the other like gun shots
from a rifle. And I could hear their feet following me up
the stairs to the porch right behind me. Very silent. I was
leading them sort of and I was only about ten years old. I
got to the top of the stairs and I was standing on the
porch. I was the first one there and I turned to see them
and they all looked right at me. All staggered because of
the steps, and all their eyes staring right at me. I saw them
like that just for a second, and then do you know what I
did little boy? I spit on the very top step just before my
father stepped down. And just as he stepped on that little
spot of spit that had nothing dirtier in it than cotton candy
and caramel apple, my whole family burst into noise like
you never heard. And my father took off his belt that he'd
just bought at the county fair. A black leather belt with a
silver buckle and a picture of Trigger engraved on the
front. And my father took one more step to the top of the
porch with the belt hanging down from his right hand and
the buckle clinking on the cement. Then he swung his arm
around slowly behind his back so that the belt dragged

through the air following his wrist and came back so fast that all I could hear was a crack as it hit my ankles and knees and I fell. Then they were silent again and waited there on the steps until my father put the belt back through the loops and buckled the buckle and hitched his jeans up over his hips. Then they all went into the house in a line. My father first, my mother second, my sisters and brothers third. And I stayed there in a ball, all rolled up, with my knees next to my chin and my hands rubbing my ankles. And I felt very good that they'd left me there by myself. (*The telephone rings: the* BOY *picks up the receiver and answers.*)

BOY: Hello. What? How did you know where I was.

SALEM: Who is it?

KENT (*from behind the door, yelling*): Salem! I do have diarrhoea after all!

BOY (*to the telephone*): If I told you it wouldn't make any difference. What difference? I'm in a hotel somewhere. Why don't you leave me alone.

SALEM: Your papa?

BOY: Or else what. You threaten me with what. Warm Coca Cola? Refried beans? Wormy corn? A hammock at night?

SALEM: Your mama?

BOY: I have air conditioning and two Rolls Royces. Match that, baby.

SALEM. Your sisters and brothers?

KENT: Salem!

BOY: Later, man. Tell it to the old lady. I'm out here on my own. Adios. (*He hangs up the phone and stands: he turns to* SALEM.)

SALEM: Your papa, right? He wants to know where you are? (*The* BOY *crosses up to the stage right bed and feels the mattress, then takes off his pants and climbs into the bed and gets under the sheets.*)

KENT: Salem! I won't be able to move!

SALEM: Now you're in muy mucho trouble, kid.

BOY: What do you know about trouble, mom?

SALEM: Mom?

BOY: You ever had Mexican ranchers ride into your village at two in the morning and kill your father and steal your sisters and brothers for working in the fields for twelve hours a day for a bowl of soup. Lord have mercy.

SALEM: That sounds like a movie.

BOY: I was in a movie once.

SALEM: Yeah?

BOY: I had to follow this cat around with a palm fan while he scored on all the native chicks.

SALEM: Did he ride a horse?

BOY: How do you score chicks on a horse?

SALEM: Well he could get off now and then.

BOY: You mean he rides from village to village and leaves the broads pregnant, and then the doctor comes around and asks them who the man was, and they all say: "I don't know. He never told me his name," and then you hear this, "Hi Yo Silver! Away!" in the distance?

SALEM: Maybe.

BOY: No, this guy was very cool. He wore linen shirts and hand-made Campeche boots and one of those straight brimmed Panamanian hats and a pistol with abalone plates on the handle. And nobody bugged him because they never knew what he was really like, you dig? Like a jaguar or an ocelot. They look very together and calm. Like you could walk up to one and just pet him gently on the nose and feel his silky fur, but you don't do that because they have something else going on that you're not sure about. Something hidden somewhere. Well this cat was like that and even moved like a jaguar. You know, sort of slinky. He hardly ever talked, and when he did it was like a rumble, like a purr.

KENT (*still behind the door*): Salem! It's getting worse! It's very, very loose!

SALEM: So what did he do?

BOY: Who?

SALEM: The guy with the linen shirts.

BOY: That's what I'm saying. He didn't have to *do* anything. He just sat around and did his stick and everything was taken care of. No worry about a place to sack out. No worry about food or booze. And when he felt like splitting he just took off. But the movie was a drag because they forced him to blow his cool at the end.

SALEM: How?

BOY: What difference. They just did. In real life he never would. I mean a cat like that doesn't get all turned around when some villager make a wisecrack about his hat.

SALEM: That's what happened?

BOY: Yeah. This fool walked up and told him his hat made him look like a clown or something like that and the cat fell right into a trap where the villagers tore him up and ate him alive. Like cannibalism or something.

SALEM: Then what happened?

BOY: All the women committed suicide.

SALEM: Really?

BOY: Yeah. But that's what I want to be like, mom. Except I wouldn't blow my cool. Not about a hat anyway. A hat's just something you wear to keep off the sun. One hat's as good as another. You blow your cool about other shit. Like when a man spits in your face.

(KENT *enters from the stage right door dressed in a straight brimmed Panamanian hat, a linen shirt, hand-made boots, underwear, and a pistol around his waist. His skin is now pale white and should appear made up. He crosses centre stage, strutting.*)

KENT: Well! I feel like a new man after all that. I think I finally flushed that old amoeba right down the old drain.

(*He struts up and down, hitching his pistol on his hips.*)

BOY: Ole!

KENT: Yes, sir! Nothing like a little amoebic dysentery to build up a man's immunity to his environment. That's the trouble with the States you know. Everything's so clean and pure and immaculate up there that a man doesn't even have a chance to build up his own immunity. They're breeding a bunch of lily-livered weaklings up there simply by not having a little dirty water around to toughen people up. Before you know it them people ain't going to be able to travel nowhere outside their own country on account of their low resistance. An isolated land of purification. That's what I'd call it. Now they got some minds. I'll grant you that. But the mind ain't nothing without the old body tagging alone behind to follow things through. And the old body ain't nothing without a little amoeba.

SALEM: Bravo!

(SALEM *and* BOY *hum,* "*When Johnny Comes Marching Home*" *as* KENT *struts more proudly up and down and takes out the pistol and starts twirling it on his trigger finger.*)

KENT: Yes, sir! That's always been true as long as man's been around on this earth and it ain't going to stop just on account of a few high falootin' ideas about comfort and leisure. No sirree! Why it's get so bad up there that even foreigners won't be able to come in on account of they won't be able to take the cleanliness. Their systems will act the same way in reverse. Nobody can come in and nobody can get out. An isolated land. That's what I call it.

BOY: Bravo! Bravo!

(KENT *gets more carried away with himself as they hum louder in the background.*)

KENT: Then the next step is inbreeding in a culture like that where there's no one coming in and no one getting out. Incest! Yes sirree! The land will fall apart. Just take your Indians for example. Look what's happened to them through incest. Smaller and smaller! Shorter life span! Rotten teeth! Low resistance! The population shrinks. The people die away. Extinction! Destruction! Rot and ruin! I see it all now clearly before me! The Greatest Society on its way downhill.

(SALEM *and* BOY *stop humming.* KENT *blows imaginary smoke out of the pistol and puts it back in the holster, he sees the* BOY *in his bed and screams.*)

KENT: What's he doing in my bed!

(*He faints on the floor.* SALEM *screams and jumps out of bed, she rushes to* KENT *and feels his wrists and slaps his face, she rushes to the telephone downstage and dials. The* BOY *just sits in bed watching,*)

SALEM: He's fainted! He's completely out! All because of your dirty water. Is there a doctor in this town?

BOY: I don't know. Isn't that what the big daddy bear said when he saw Goldilocks? What's he doing in my bed, mothafucka?

SALEM (*on the phone*): Hello. Can you get me a doctor right away? Oh shit. Puede un doctor quiere muy- muy- (*To the* BOY.) Can you tell him? Please. Tell him I need a doctor. Tell him it's dysentery. Please. I don't speak very well.

BOY: Pardone me no habla español.

SALEM: Thanks, son. Hello, Puede quiere un doctor de medecina muy pronto aqui! Comprende! No, no, no. Un doctor de medecina. Si! Pronto por favor. Muchas gracias. No, no! Mi esposo es muy enfermo para la turista. Sabe? Bueno. Muchas gracias.

(*She hangs up the phone and rushes back to* KENT, *she slaps his face again and feels his wrists.*)

BOY (*still sitting in bed*): They say the white of an egg is good for poisoning.

SALEM: Just shut up. He's got the trots.

BOY: You force about half a dozen egg whites down the throat and then they vomit up the poison. It's very easy. They use it on dogs even.

SALEM: Look, sonny, you just sit tight and don't say another word, or I'll call the chief of police and have them take you back to your mommy and daddy. What he needs is a wet towel. A cold wet towel.

(*She crosses to the stage right door and goes inside, closing the door behind her.*)

BOY: A wet towel is working from the outside in! With poison you have to work from the inside out!

SALEM (*behind the door*): It's not poison!

(*A loud knock on the stage left door.*)

SALEM (*behind the door*): That must be the doctor! Would you answer it, please! I'll pay you for it!

BOY: I don't have any pants on!

SALEM (*behind the door*): Well put them on for Christ's sake!

BOY: Yes, mam. 'Scuse me, mam.

(*He jumps out of bed and puts his pants back on, another loud* knock at the stage left door.)

Be right with you, boss. Just as fast as I can. Yes sir. Just hold tight for Jesus sake. We got a busy house here what with the master sick and all.

SALEM: Hurry up!

BOY: Yes, mam. Right away, mam.

(*He goes to the stage left door and opens it. There are a* WITCH-DOCTOR *and his* SON *standing in the door: they are both very dark skinned. The* SON *looks exactly like the* BOY *and is dressed the same way. The* WITCH-DOCTOR *is dressed in sandals, short black pants, a bright red shirt, a short black jacket with elaborate floral designs on the sleeves and the back, a purple bandana wrapped around his head like a turban with tassels hanging down the back. He has two live chickens tied by the feet and hanging upside down from each of his wrists: he carries a long rope whip in one hand, a long machete hangs from his belt. The* SON *carries a burlap bag full of incense, firecrackers, and candles in one hand, and in the other is a large coffee can full of burning incense, strung with a long leather thong: he swings the can back and forth by the thong so that the smoke from the incense rises. They cross the centre stage. At all times they should behave as though they have nothing to do with the play and just happen to be there.*)

BOY: The doctor is here, mam! Shall I show him in?

SALEM (*behind the door*): Show him where Kent is and tell him I'll be right there!

BOY (*motioning to* KENT): Doctor, this is Kent. Kent is very sick from poisoning and needs your help.

DOCTOR (*crouching down next to* KENT): Pason!

BOY: Si.

SON: Pason!

DOCTOR: Pason! Aeey!

BOY: Si.

(*The* WITCH-DOCTOR *rises slowly and motions to his* SON *to set down the bag and the incense can, then he motions to the two suitcases on the floor. The* SON *goes to each suitcase and carries them over to* KENT, *who remains limp on the floor through all this. The* SON *then opens each suitcase and dumps the contents all over* KENT*: these should be money and various tourist items. The* WITCH-DOCTOR*, at the same time, crosses centre stage and sets the chickens on the floor: he then picks up the incense can and waves it several times over the chickens, crossing himself as he does this: he crosses to* KENT *and does the same thing with him and then whips* KENT *across the back several times with the rope. He goes through the same actions over and over again, crossing from the chickens to* KENT*, and then back to the chickens, while the* SON *takes out incense from the burlap bag and places it in small metal bowls, also from the bag, in a circle all around* KENT*. Then he lights each bowl of incense very methodically and crosses himself as he does this: then he goes to the bag again and takes out candles: he places the candles also in a circle around* KENT *and lights each one as he did with the incense: after this is finished he goes to the bag and takes out a string of firecrackers and lights it at* KENT'*s feet. All during this, they chant these words over and over in any order they want to; "Quetzal, Totzal, Cobal, Pason." They can repeat each word several times or say them in series: the whole thing should be very habitual and appear as though they'd done it a thousand times before. They should now and then look at the audience and wonder why it's there, as they go through the motions. Meanwhile, the* BOY *crosses to the downstage apron and talks directly to the audience, as a tourist guide speaking to tourists. He crosses casually back and forth.* SALEM *remains behind the stage right door.*)

BOY: The people in this area speak the purest Mayan existing today. The language has changed only slightly since the days of the great Mayan civilization before the time of the conquest. It's even more pure than the Mayan spoken by the primitive Lacandones, who live in the state of Chiapas. It's even purer by far than the Mayan spoken in the Yucatan, where much Spanish and Ladino admixtures have been added. In short, it's very pure and nearly impossible for an outsider to learn, although many have tried.

SALEM (*still behind the door*): Tell him to do whatever he has to!

Don't worry about the money!

BOY: The man here is the most respected of all, or I should say, his profession is. But then, we can't separate a man from his profession, can we? Anyway, there are several witch-doctors for each tribe and they become this through inheritance only. In other words, no one is elected to be a witch-doctor. This would be impossible since there is so very much to learn and the only way to learn it is to be around a witch-doctor all the time. Therefore the witch-doctor's oldest son, whom you see here, will fall heir to his father's position. He listens carefully and watches closely to everything his father does and even helps out in part of the ceremony as you see here. A great kid.

SALEM: Tell him that I'm sick too and may need some help!

BOY: The people of the village are very superstitious and still believe in spirits possessing the body. They believe that in some way the evil spirits must be driven from the body in order for the body to become well again. This is why you see the witch-doctor beating the man. This is to drive the evil spirits out. The firecrackers are to scare them away. The incense smoke, or copal, as it's called here, is to send the prayers up to the god. They believe the smoke will carry the prayers to heaven. The candles are so that the god will look down and see the light and know that there's somebody praying down here, since the god only looks when something attracts his attention.

SALEM: I think I've got the same thing?

BOY: Although there are several European doctors in town, the people will not go to them for help. Instead they call for the witch-doctor who comes to their home and prays for them and beats them up and then goes to the top of the mountain where the god of health is supposed to be. There is an idol there that the witch-doctor prays to in much the same way as you see here. Please don't try to go to the top of the mountain alone though, without a guide, because it can be very dangerous. Last year a group of students from an American university went up there and tried to steal the idol for an anthropological study and they were almost killed. It's perfectly safe with a guide though, and you can always find me in front of the pharmacy. Or just ask someone for Sebastian Smith.

SALEM: It's getting worse now! It's very, very loose!

BOY: Of course, in the days before Christ, they used to sacrifice young girls to the gods. But now that's been made illegal by the government so the people use chickens instead. That's what the two chickens are for. They usually give the poor chicken a little drink of cane liquor to deaden the pain but sometimes they don't even bother. You'll notice a slight mixture of Catholic ritual incorporated into the pagan rites. This has become more and more apparent within the last century but the people still hold firmly to their primitive beliefs.

SALEM: Ask him if he can come in here as soon as he's done with Kent!

BOY: The marriage is fixed by the family, and the partners have nothing to say in this matter. The girls begin having babies at the age of fourteen and usually have about fifteen children before they die. The average life expectancy is thirty-eight for women and forty-two for men. The women hold equal property rights as the men and get paid a salary by the men for each baby they have. The eldest son in each family always falls heir to the father's property. The puberty rites for boys are very stringent here and vary all the way from having the thumbnail on the right hand peeled away to having three small incisions made with a razor on the end of the penis. By the time the penis has healed they believe the boy has become a man.

SALEM: Tell him to hurry! It's getting much worse!

(*At this time, the* SON *takes all of* KENT's *clothes off except his underwear, and piles them neatly at his feet, while the* WITCH-DOCTOR *takes out his machete and waves it over the chicken. He also swings the coffee can back and forth and chants more intensely.*)

BOY: At this time the clothes are removed from the man in preparation for the sacrifice. The chickens will be decapitated and their bodies held over the man to allow the blood to drop on to his back. This will allow the good spirits to enter his body and make him well again. The clothes will be burned since it is believed that the evil spirits still reside in his clothes. And if anyone should put them on they would have bad health for the rest of their days and die within two years.

SALEM: I can't stand it any more!

BOY: After this, the witch-doctor will pray over the heads of the chickens and then take them to the top of the mountain, where he will throw them into the fire and then do some more praying. Now is the time for the sacrifice. For those of you who aren't used to this sort of thing you may close your eyes and just listen, or else you could keep in mind that it's not a young girl but a dumb chicken.

(*The* SON *goes to the chickens and stretches their necks out on the floor. The* WITCH-DOCTOR *cuts off both their heads with one stroke of his machete.* SALEM *screams from the bathroom.*)

SALEM: Oh my God!

(*The* WITCH-DOCTOR *takes both the chicken bodies and holds them over* KENT *so that they bleed on his back. The* SON *chants over the heads and crosses himself: the* WITCH-DOCTOR *also chants.* SALEM *enters from the bathroom: her skin is pale white now: she clutches her stomach and goes in circles around the stage in great pain.*)

BOY: Why, madame, your sunburn is gone.

SALEM: I'm sick and pale, and dying from the same thing as Kent. What's happened to Kent? How is my Kent? How is my boy?

BOY: He's dead.

SALEM: No, he's not dead. I'm not dead and I have the same thing. The same rotten thing.

BOY: You're both dead.

(*The* SON *and the* WITCH-DOCTOR *continue to chant and stay in their positions watching* SALEM *and the* BOY, *but remaining uninvolved.* SALEM *goes in circles and paces back and forth clutching her stomach.*)

SALEM: Don't tell me that. I wish I was dead but I'm not. Don't tell me that now when I need comfort and soothing. When I need an alcohol rub down and some hot lemonade. How can you speak to me in this way. I'm having cold chills. My body is burning alive. How will I make it back to my home?

BOY: Plane or train or bus or car.

SALEM: Don't tell me that now. Look at me sweat. Who's around who knows what to do? Who is there?

BOY: The doctor's right here.

(SALEM *becomes more and more delirious, clutching her stomach and head.*)

SALEM: I'm seeing things in front of my eyes. I'm shaking all over. Look at me shaking. What's going on! My eyes are popping out of my head.

BOY: You could lie down. Kent's lying down.

SALEM: Kent's faking. Kent's playing dead while I'm the one who needs attention. Look at me now. Just look. Don't look at him.

BOY: I see.

SALEM: No, you don't. You said I was dead so you must see a corpse. Now I'm getting scared, you know.

BOY: How come?

SALEM: You wouldn't understand. Look at me. I'm not even dressed.

(*The* BOY *crosses and picks up off the floor a Mexican poncho that was one of the items in the suitcase and hands it to* SALEM, *who keeps pacing up and down.*)

BOY: You can wear this.

SALEM: No, no. I need something like a nice wool sweater and some nice cotton slacks and a nice big bracelet and some jade ear-rings and some nice warm shoes. And I need to have my hair all done and my nails fixed up and someone to take me out to dinner.

BOY: Well wear this, mom, and as soon as daddy's well, we'll all go out to dinner.

SALEM: All right. All right. But don't call me names.

(*She puts on the poncho and then continues to pace as the* BOY *crosses to* KENT *and feels his head. The* WITCH-DOCTOR *and his* SON *continue to chant.*)

SALEM: I feel so silly.

BOY: Don't feel silly. They keep you very warm. It's what the natives wear.

SALEM: Not about that. I feel silly because I'm sick and cold, and Kent's very sick, and I'm not sure at all about what I should do, about who I should ask about what I should do. I don't speak and I'm not from here.

BOY: Ask me. I've been around.

SALEM: Around where, for instance? Around what? You've got built-in immunity. Just look at me. I'm almost naked. (*The* BOY *begins to put on each item of* KENT's *costume as they continue.*)

BOY: Better than being too weighted down with extra junk you don't need. Just take a canteen, some sandwiches.

SALEM: Take them where? I'm staying here. You're the one who's got to leave. We rented this room, Kent and me. *We're* on vacation, *you're* not.

BOY: Good. I hope you have a nice trip back.

SALEM: Not back! Here! We've just come here! We're not going back now! You can see Kent lying there dead and at the same time tell me I should have a nice trip back? I can tell you it won't be so nice!

BOY: Well, I hope you have a nice time here then.

SALEM: Put down those clothes! Get out of this room before I call the police.

BOY: Someone pulled out the phone.

SALEM: I don't care! I want you to leave.

BOY: You'll need me around to translate. To run downstairs to the pharmacy and get what you need.

SALEM: What will I need?

BOY: Well, you'll need sterile white gauze and tubes of green ointment and different kinds of hot and cold salve. And you'll need ice packs and painkillers and iodine and stimulants and penicillin pills.

SALEM: I haven't been gored by a bull. I've been screwed by amoeba and I don't even know what they look like. They probably have little white heads and red eyes and two legs, but I know they don't go on for ever.

BOY: They'll follow you around wherever you go.

SALEM: Don't try to scare me, sonny. I've been around. You
don't know the first thing about amoeba. You could eat
chile right off the street and not catch a thing. It's me who's
in danger, not you. So don't give me advice. Look how
strong you are. Just look. Now look at me.

BOY: Well, how do I look?

SALEM: Come up here, boy, and stand straight. Come on up
here! Come on! Come on! Come up here with me and let's
see what you look like now that you've grown.
(*The* BOY *crosses up to her, now fully dressed in* KENT'S
costume. SALEM *takes him by the hand and leads him downstage centre: she leads him back and forth by the hand
downstage and speaks to the audience as though it were a
market-place full of villagers. The chanting gets louder in the
background.*)
Mira! Mira! Mira! Look what is here! Look what I have
for you! For any of you who has the right price! Quantos
pesos por el niño! El niño es muy bravo no! Si! He has
come to me from the hills with his father's clothes and his
mother's eyes! Look at his hands! How strong! How brave!
His father says he is old enough now to work for himself!
To work for one of you! To work hard and long! His
father has given him over to me for the price of six hogs!
I give him to you now for the price of twelve! Doce paygar
por el niño aqui! Come on! Come on! No?
(*She drags the* BOY *by the hand, down off the edge of the
stage into the audience, and walks up and down the aisles
showing the* BOY *to the people and yelling loudly. The*
WITCH-DOCTOR *and his* SON *watch* SALEM *and the* BOY *in the
same way the audience does, and in some way reflect the
audience's reaction back to them, but go on with their
chanting.* KENT *remains limp.*)
Quantos pesos por el niño! Quantos! Quantos! What more
could you want? At this time in his life, he is worth more
to you than all the ponchos you could make in three
months. In four months! He'll bring in your sheep at night!

He'll take them out in the morning! He'll scare away dogs
and crows and cut up your corn! Feel his calves and
thighs! Look at his eyes and his mouth! He's honest too!
He'll never steal or lie or cheat! He also sings songs from
his native tribe and carves wooden animals in his spare
time! He'll speak to you only when he's spoken to and
he'll never ever laugh behind your back! He's trained to
haul wood and carry water up to thirty miles without
resting once! What more could you want? What more
could you ask? You can always re-sell him, you know.
And you'll never get less than six hogs! His skin is clean!
He has no scars! Probably cleaner skin than any of yours!
His hair is free of lice and ticks! He has all his teeth! What
are you waiting for? How much will you pay? Cuantos!
Cuantos! You'll never get another chance! How much will
you pay for this boy?
(*The phone suddenly begins to ring.* SALEM *and the* BOY *stop
immediately and turn to the stage: they are in the centre
aisle at the back of the theatre. The* SON *and the* WITCH-
DOCTOR *stop chanting and just stare at the phone as it rings:
the* SON *slowly crosses up to the phone and answers it.*)

SON: Hello. What? (*He holds one hand over the receiver and
yells to the* BOY.) It's for you! (*The* BOY *crosses down the
aisle toward the phone.* SALEM *remains where she is.*)

SALEM: Tell them you're going away on a trip. Tell them you're
going to the U.S.A.! Tell them whatever they want to
hear!
(*The* BOY *takes the phone from the* SON *and answers it. The*
SON *goes back to the* WITCH-DOCTOR *and they both begin
chanting quietly over* KENT'*s body again. The lights slowly
begin to fade at this point: also the fan begins to die down.*)

BOY (*on the phone*): Bueno. Si. Si. Esta bien. No. Si. Volver a
la casa. Si. Si. En esta noche. No. No me gusta. Si. Esta
bien. No. Esta mejor.

SALEM: What do they want! Tell them you're going with me!
(*She begins to slowly cross down the aisle towards the stage
now.*)

BOY: Estoy muy triste aqui. So. Bueno. Tu tambien? Bueno.

Hasta luego. So, Buena noche papa. Adios.

(*He hangs up the phone and stares at* SALEM, *who crosses slowly toward him up the aisle. The* WITCH-DOCTOR *and his* SON *just stand staring at* KENT *and chanting softly. The lights keep fading.* KENT *remains on the floor.*)

BOY: That's my father.

SALEM: Your father is dead. You're going with me. We have more things to do.

BOY: That's the first time he ever speaks on a phone in his life. He says to start walking down the road toward my home and he'll start walking toward me, and we'll meet half-way and embrace.

SALEM: How will you meet in the dark? You can't even see the road.

BOY: We'll meet in the light. My home is far from here. We'll meet as the sun come up. We'll see each other from very far off and we'll look to each other like dwarfs. He'll see me, and I'll see him, and we'll get bigger and bigger as we approach.

SALEM: You and your father will die in your hut. You could come with me. I could teach you how to drive a car. We could go everywhere together.

BOY: Then we'll tell about where we've been, and I'll sing songs that he's never heard.

SALEM: Your father is deaf!

(*She gets closer to the* BOY *as the lights get dimmer.*)

BOY: And we'll sit together and smoke by the side of the road, until a truck come by heading toward my home. And my father will kiss me good-bye and climb on the back and drive off, and I'll wait for another truck going the other way. A pale blue truck with a canvas back, carrying chickens and goats, and a small picture of the Madonna on the dashboard, and green plastic flowers hanging from the rear view mirror, and golden tassels and fringe around the window, and striped tape wrapped around the gear shift and the steering wheel, and a drunk driver with a long black beard, and the radio turned up as loud as it goes and singing Spanish as we drive out into the Gulf of Mexico and float to the other side.

SALEM: You'll never make it alive!

(*The lights dim out and the fan stops as* SALEM *reaches the* BOY.)

ACT TWO

SCENE. *The set is organized exactly the same as Act I except the impression this time is that of an American hotel room. All the colour is gone from Act I and replaced by different shades of shiny tan and grey. The signs on each door are in English and read "BATHROOM" and "PLEASE DO NOT DISTURB" in black and white. The telephone is plastic. The fan is gone. The suitcases at the foot of each bed are matching plastic.* KENT *is in the stage right bed propped up by pillows and sleeping with a thermometer hanging out of his mouth. He wears long underwear.* SALEM *is in the bathroom. She wears American plastic clothes. The lights come up fast. Loud knocks on the stage left door.* KENT *remains asleep.* SALEM *comes out of the bathroom and crosses to the door. She opens it and* DOC, *played by the actor who played* WITCH-DOCTOR, *is standing in the doorway with his son,* SONNY, *played by the actor who played* BOY. DOC *is dressed like a country doctor from Civil War times, with boots, a coat with tails, string tie, suspenders, a pistol carried in a shoulder holster, wide-brimmed black hat, and a large black satchel with supplies.* SONNY *is dressed exactly the same as* DOC *but without the satchel and pistol.*

SALEM: Oh good. Finally. Come in. You *are* the ones from the clinic?

(*They both enter.*)

DOC: Yes, mam. (*Takes off his hat.* SONNY *follows suit.*)

SALEM: You brought help? You didn't have to bring help. It's nothing serious.

DOC: No, mam. This here's my boy, Sonny.

SALEM: How do you do?

SONNY: All right.

DOC: He's tagging along. Learning the trade. Apprenticeship, you know.

SALEM: Well, there he is.

DOC: Let's have a look.

(*He crosses to* KENT *and sits beside him, checking his eyes, forehead, etc., as he talks.* KENT *appears to sleep through this.* SONNY *and* SALEM *stand by.*)

SALEM: I don't know what to tell you more than what I told you over the phone.

DOC: Well you ain't told me nothing. Was my secretary or something you must a' spoke to. You ain't told me.

SALEM: Oh.

DOC: So tell me somethin'.

SALEM: Well. You mean symptoms?

DOC: Somethin'. Gotta go on somethin' when you're treatin' illness. Otherwise you might as well be treatin' health.

SALEM: Well. He goes in cycles.

DOC: Cycles?

SALEM: Yes. One thing and then another.

(*Through this,* DOC *motions* SONNY *to open up his satchel and hand him different instruments for checking the heart, eyes, ears, mouth, etc.* DOC *goes through these procedures, while* SALEM *paces around.*)

DOC: From what to what?

SALEM: From sleep to being awake.

DOC: Me too.

SONNY: Same here.

SALEM: No. No. Not like him. It's not the same. We're talking about something. We'll be talking back and forth and we'll be not necessarily deeply involved in what we're saying, but nevertheless talking. And he'll gradually begin to go away.

DOC: How do you mean?

SALEM: You'll see a person. Like you're seeing me now, and I'm talking to you, and you're talking to me, and gradually something happens to me while we're talking, until I disappear.

DOC: He leaves the room?

SALEM: No, he falls asleep. Like now. He's sleeping. But before you came, he was talking to me. Now he's asleep.

DOC: Now look here, mam. I need things like runny nose, aching back, itchy skin, bloody urine, runny bowels. Things like that.

SALEM: They aren't there. What's there is what you see. Sleeping. I thought it was just fatigue, so we came here to rest and get strong. But it's worse than that. I can tell.

DOC: How?

SALEM: By the way you look.

SONNY (*spoken in one breath*): You shouldn't worry, mam. Pa looks like that always when he's checking to see what's wrong. Honest. All the time. And I should know, since I'm always around when he's checking to see what's wrong, and you're not always around. In fact this is the first time ever you've been able to see Pa in action. So you should trust me and him and not yourself.

SALEM: I know doctors. I've been around doctors and they change faces. They have different faces that tell you what's what. And I can tell what's what from the face he has on. So don't tell me.

DOC: You'll have to tell me somethin' more, mam, to speed things up.

SONNY: The more we know the faster we can get to work.

SALEM: What do you mean? Do you help? You're not a doctor.

DOC: Look lady, no more dilly dally.

SALEM: I'm trying to concentrate.

SONNY: Don't try. You can't concentrate if you try.

SALEM: Boy! You should be a doctor, Sonny. You have all this valuable information up your sleeve.

SONNY: I do my best.

DOC: Symptoms, man, symptoms.

SALEM: Symptoms!

SONNY: Things that show on the outside what the inside might be up to.

SALEM: I know, I know. Yawning. A lot of yawning, and then a lot of talking, then more yawning and talking, and finally sleep, and then waking and talking and yawning and sleep again. Over and over.

(DOC *stands abruptly.*)

DOC: I have it! Of course!

SALEM: What?

DOC: We must wake him up immediately. Right now, before it's too late. Help me.

(He and SONNY *pull* KENT *out of bed and stand him up.* KENT *remains asleep.)*

SALEM: What is it?

DOC: Your husband, mam, is subject to what we call chronic Encephalitis Lethargica, also known as sleepy sickness and as Epidemic Encephalitis, von Economo's Disease. A disease that appears from time to time, especially in spring, in the form of epidemics.

SONNY: See there. I told ya'.

*(*SONNY *and* DOC *slap* KENT's *face and begin pacing him around the room as they talk to* SALEM. KENT *slowly comes out of sleep into a groggy stupor.* DOC *crosses to his satchel and leaves* SONNY *pacing with* KENT. *He pulls out a medical chart from his satchel and unrolls it: the chart is a nude photograph of* KENT, *with labels and diagrams illustrating encephalitis. He hangs it on the upstage wall as he continues to talk. He points to different sections of the chart with a marker as he gives the speech, like an ageing college professor who can't remember his lecture.)*

DOC: It is a virus infection, attacking chiefly the basal ganglia, the cerebrum, and the brain stem. These undergo dropsical swelling, haemorrhages, and, ultimately, destruction of areas of tissue involving both nerve-cells and fibres. The process may involve other parts of the brain, the spinal cord, and even other organs.

SALEM: Oh no.

DOC: The illness begins, usually, with rise of temperature and increasing drowsiness or lethargy, which may gradually proceed to a state of complete unconsciousness. In some cases, however, the patient, instead of being drowsy, passes at first through a stage of restlessness, which may amount to maniacal excitement. As a rule, the drowsiness deepens gradually over a period of a week or more, and accompanying it there appears various forms of paralysis, shown by drooping of the eyelids, squint, and weakness of one or both sides of the face. The nerves controlling the muscles of the throat are also sometimes paralysed, causing changes in the voice and difficulty in swallowing. In some cases the disease affects the spinal cord, producing severe pain in one or more of the limbs, and it is frequently followed by partial paralysis. Signs of inflammation are not infrequently found in other organs, and haemorrhages may be visible beneath the skin and in the muscles, or blood may be vomited up or passed in the stools. The effects last usually for many months; the patient remains easily tired and somnolent, or frequently showing rigidity of muscle, mask-like faces, festinant gait, and rhythmical coarse tremors, resembling the clinical picture of paralysis agitans and known in epidemic encephalitis as Parkinsonism. Other cases show a considerable resemblance in symptoms to chorea, and still others to the disease known as general paralysis; and many cases which result in physical recovery are left with profoundly deteriorated mental powers.

SALEM: I knew he was sick. What'll we do? We were on our way to Mexico, doctor. To give him a rest.

SONNY: A rest?

SALEM: Yes. I mean to get him better.

DOC: There is no specific treatment for the disease, but he must be kept in motion and, if possible, induced to talk. The more motion the better, lest it prove fatal. Benzedrine sulphate is also useful in some patients at this stage.

SALEM: Do you have some?

DOC: Sure do. You take his arm, mam, with Sonny, and walk him up and down while I get the pills. Keep him moving at all cost.

(*She follows his instructions while* DOC *gets a bottle of pills out of his satchel.* KENT *is yawning.*)

SALEM: What a thing to have. It sounds just terrible. And we were on our way for a vacation.

(*When* KENT *speaks he is in a world unrelated to anything on stage, even when he talks to the other actors and even when his dialogue seems coherent to the action around him.*)

KENT: Haa! Your hands are something, boy. Fast hands.

SONNY: He talks.

DOC: Good, good. Keep him going. Keep him talking.

KENT: Don't have screwy knuckles like that just playing hand ball or something. Hand ball you use the palm. But bloody knuckles. Wowee.

SALEM: What?

DOC: Don't worry. Give him these when you get a chance, but let him talk.

SALEM: What are they?

DOC: Benzedrine. Just keep him going.
    (*He hands* SALEM *the pills, then crosses to the stage left bed and takes off his coat and sits on the bed with his hands clasped behind his head, and watches.* KENT *paces, with* SONNY *and* SALEM *holding on to his arms.*)

KENT: Just don't worry. It carries me through.

SALEM: Shouldn't you be doing something else for him, doctor? What are you doing now?

SONNY. You should let Pa alone now, mam. It's up to us to carry through with what he says.

DOC: Just keep him movin'.

SALEM: What are *you* doing?

DOC: Thought I'd take a snooze here for a bit. It's been a long ride out.
    (*He closes his eyes and begins to sleep, as* SONNY *and* SALEM *keep* KENT *pacing.*)

SALEM: Great. You're doing nothing.

SONNY. It was quite a ride, mam.

SALEM: What do I care about your ride. You're *supposed* to ride when you have a sick patient. Doctors have been riding for years. Back and forth. Wherever they're needed, they go. They even have to swear that they'll do it before they can——

KENT: How should anyone know. They get thrown into it.

SALEM (*to* DOC): Listen, is he eventually supposed to come out of it, or do we just keep this up for ever? Hey!

SONNY: Shh! He's asleep, mam.

SALEM: Well how are we going to tell when he's all right?

SONNY: Pa will give the sign.

SALEM: But he's asleep.

SONNY: He wakes up every half-hour on the hour, then goes back to sleep.

SALEM: How come?

SONNY: He used to raise puppies. They have to be fed once every half-hour until they're at least nine weeks old.

KENT: A doctor shouldn't fall asleep on the job.

SALEM: That's right. What is he, a veterinarian?

SONNY: If he's on the job and he's too tired to do the job justice, then he should fall asleep and wake up rested to do a good job.

SALEM: Do you want some puppies, Kent?

SONNY: Not yet.

(*They keep pacing with* KENT, *while* DOC *sleeps. The pacing should change back and forth, from* KENT *pulling them along, to them pulling* KENT *along: it should cover the entire stage and continually change speed and quality. At no time do* SONNY *and* SALEM *let go of his arms.*)

KENT: I know that type. That sneaky type. That member of the horror show who disappears into it when he doesn't want to be seen, and then pops out when he does.

SALEM: I don't know how to talk to him.

SONNY: Just relax. Let him do the talking.

KENT: That type came to our door once, with my family inside, where they always were. Watching horror shows on —— The monster's always a nice guy. Notice that. Always nice.

SALEM: Kent! Wake up.

SONNY: Shh. Let him go.

SALEM: But we were going to Mexico.

KENT: So he knocks on the door, and Pa answers it, and the guy comes in with a brief case. Right into the house. And the house is in the middle of the prairie, with nothing around but prairie and one huge factory where they make something inside that you never see outside. All you can see is smoke coming out. And he comes in, with Ma and brothers and sisters all around chewing on the furniture, and Pa dying for a smoke.

(DOC *yawns, then begins snoring loudly.*)

SALEM: Doctor! Do something!

KENT: Shh! And Pa can hardly walk from lack of everything he needs. So the guy from the factory sits down next to Pa, who's dying, and says to him I see you've got all these lovely sons and daughters, and Pa nods. Then the guy from the horror show says and I see they're all dying, and Ma nods. And the guy says I know you never get a chance to see inside our factory, to see what exactly it is that we make, and they shake their heads. So right now I'm going to give you a chance, and he opens up the briefcase which is loaded with different packs of cigarettes. Pa smiles and licks his nose. The kids gather around. Ma faints. The guy says I'm going to make you a little offer, my friend.

SONNY: Pa!

KENT: If you change each one of the stupid names you gave your eight kids, from whatever it is now, to one of the eight brand names of our cigarettes, I'll set you up in your own little business and give you all the smokes you need. So don't go shoving benzedrine in my face.

SALEM: It's for your own good, Kent.

SONNY: Pa! I think we need help.

KENT: You're doing fine. You don't even have to hold on. The pace is great.

SONNY: Don't believe him, mam. They all say that. And just at the point when they say that, you know that the last thing in the world you should do is to do what they say.

SALEM: But maybe he means it. Kent? Are you O.K.?

SONNY: Just keep hold a' that arm, lady. Do exactly the opposite of whatever he wants. Believe me. I've learned.

KENT: You're no doctor.

SONNY: Last week Pa and I were out at the Tuttle farm, out past Lansingville, to see old lady Tuttle, since her neighbours called us up and asked us to go give her a look-see, since she was doing a lot of fiddle playin' late at night and they was all worried. So we rode out there about 3 a.m. one mornin' last week, thinkin' we'd catch her at it

if she was really doin' what they said she was doin', and
she was all right. She was doin' it.

SALEM: Look, we have to get him well so we can get started on
our trip.

SONNY: Sittin' out there on her front porch just as plain as day.
Tappin' her foot and rockin' to the tune she was doin'.
Think it was, "Hang Toad's Got No Stock In My Mind".
Somethin' like that.

SALEM: Doctor!

SONNY: So we sneak up on her through the shrub pine and sit
there in the dark for a spell just listenin' to that fine old
fiddle a' Mrs. Tuttle's.
(DOC *wakes up suddenly and sits up on the bed: he stands
abruptly and puts on his coat: he checks his watch. The rest
keep pacing.*)

DOC: What!

ONNY: Just tellin' the lady here about old lady Tuttle, Pa.
(DOC *gets involved in the story and wanders downstage.*)

DUC: Oh yes. Well it was a strange night. A night the likes a'
which could make you figure old lady Tuttle was the only
one in the world to speak of, and we two, my boy and I,
we was like shrub pine. Just lookin' on. Growin' slowly.
Rooted in one place. Lettin' seasons change us. And Mrs.
Tuttle was playin' for us like she was playin' for the world
of bushes and plants and insect life.

KENT: So Pa was set up in business at last.

DOC: Shut up! Keep him still!
(*They keep pacing* KENT, *while* DOC *comes down and speaks
to the audience while walking around.*)

SALEM: Doctor.

DOC: So there we was. My boy and I, hidden from view.
Invisible to old lady Tuttle. And we noticed after a bit how
we was gettin' entranced by that darn fiddle a' hers. That
old lady had us hypnotized there for a while, until my boy
here realized it and snapped us both out of it.

SALEM: Doctor! Pay attention to your patient.

DOC: Well we figured it out between the two of us but only
after it was too late. Instead we fell right into her trap and

walked right up to her porch just as plain as you please
and——

SONNY: That's not exactly how it went, Pa.

DOC: You shut up! How it went is no concern of mine or yours.
All I want to do is finish up and go home.

KENT: And leave me stranded.

SALEM: How can a doctor leave you stranded, Kent?

DOC: By ridin' out, lady.

SALEM: I'll call the clinic.

DOC: Try it!

SONNY: Pa cut the wires on the way in, mam.

SALEM: You what! That's rotten.

DOC (*to audience*): So we walk right up to old lady Tuttle, who
doesn't even see us. Like we're not there, even.

KENT: That means that I'll fall asleep and never wake up.

SALEM: Don't be silly. We'll keep you going all night if we have
to.

KENT: What about tomorrow?

SALEM: And tomorrow we'll go to Mexico.

DOC: And the closer we get the better we see that she could be
anywhere. She couldn't care less.

KENT: Let go of me. I want to check the phone.

DOC: Don't let him go at any cost!

KENT: I want to check on the phone!
(*They keep* KENT *pacing.*)

DOC (*to audience*): There's one thing I could never stand in all
those years ridin' back and forth treatin' sores and wounds
and shrunken hands.

SONNY: What's that, Pa?

DOC: That's the absolute unwillingness that all them sickly,
misfit imbeciles had for going along with what I'd prescribe.
You say one thing and they do the exact opposite right
off the bat. Soon as you turn your back off they'd go in
the wrong direction. Straight into what I was tryin' to lead
them out of.

SALEM: Doctor! He seems to be all right now.

SONNY: Ya' gotta watch the tricks, mam. Ya' gotta develop an
eye for the tricks so you can tell one kind from another

kind.

DOC: It got a point there, in my traipsin' around, where I felt like a doctor was the last thing needed. Just let the fools work it out for themselves.

SALEM: He's moving and everything. He's talking and walking. That's what you wanted. Can't we let him go now? Doctor.

DOC: Sure! Sure enough! Let him go!

(*They all stop still.*)

SALEM: Kent?

(*The let go of* KENT's *arms and back away.* KENT *remains standing still.* DOC *crosses up to him and checks his eyelids, then steps back.*)

DOC: All right.

SALEM: What? He's all right now, isn't he?

DOC: Sure. Fit as a fiddle.

(KENT *rushes to the phone and picks it up: he tries to dial with no success: he freezes as he hangs up the phone.*)

KENT: They cut the wires. The juice.

SALEM: Kent. We can take off tomorrow if you want.

SONNY: Why Mexico? Why not Canada, where you'd be less noticeable?

SALEM: That's right, Kent. In Mexico they're all dark. They'd notice us right off the bat.

DOC: Especially with a corpse.

SONNY: They'd notice a corpse anywhere.

SALEM: What do you mean?

KENT: Not here. In Lansingville. Get a TV in here. Some sandwiches.

SALEM: No. That's silly. We want to get out, not in.

DOC: I could stop by once a week.

SALEM: Here's some pills, Kent. Take some pills. You'll be all right.

(*She hands* KENT *the pills. He holds them in his hand and remains frozen.*)

I'll get you a glass of water.

(*She exits into the bathroom.* DOC *and* SONNY *move in on* KENT, *who stays frozen.*)

SONNY: Unless ya' want to follow Pa's directions, fool, you'll never get out a' this hole.

DOC: That's right. Listen to the boy.

SONNY: He knows what he's sayin', Pa does.

DOC: Ain't been travellin' through hick town after town, tearin' the scabs off a' infection that otherwise would a' made a corpse out of a live man if the pus wasn't allowed to draw off. Ain't been doin' that and not comin' back with some savvy.

SONNY: They do it with trees too, so don't feel bad.

DOC: Just keep yourself movin', son. It's the only way out.

(SALEM *enters with a glass of water and hands it to* KENT.)

SALEM: Here, Kent.

DOC: See here, your woman's right behind ya', boy.

(KENT *takes the pills and a gulp of water: he hands the glass back to* SALEM, *then stands.*)

KENT: Well. Thanks, Doc. Hope you have a nice trip back.

DOC: Oh. Well. Nice? Sure. It won't be so nice. I mean it won't be any nicer than it was coming out.

KENT: How nice was that?

DOC: So, so.

KENT: Well, I hope it's nicer than that.

(KENT *begins wandering around freely, looking at the walls of the room.*)

SONNY: That can't be. It's always the same. Dusty, hot. Ya' get tired and rest at the same places along the road, under the same trees.

KENT: Why's that?

DOC: Well, that's where the wells are, ya' see. Ya' have to get tired where the water is so's you don't pass 'em by. Otherwise, you're just out a' luck.

KENT: Don't you carry a canteen or something?

SALEM: We can take off tomorrow then, Kent. If you feel all right.

KENT: How will you reserve tickets? The wires are cut. The juice is off.

SONNY: That's right.

DOC: Anyway we gotta hang around for a bit to check you out. Make sure ya' don't have a relapse.

KENT: A what?

DOC: A relapse. To make sure the same business doesn't start all over again.

SONNY: You need your bag, Pa?

SALEM: I could walk down the road and make a call from the pay phone.

DOC: Ya' see ya' could easily fall back into it if ya' don't watch your step. It depends on a very fragile margin in the basal ganglia. One little jar, and poof. You have to keep the opposite pole in motion in order not to activate the opposite one.

SONNY: He's right.

SALEM: Shall I go make reservations, Kent?

DOC: Not yet! He's in no shape to be wanderin' into the freezin' night the way he is. Out there with the crickets.

KENT: I think I'll stay.

SALEM: Well then I'll go.

DOC: No. You should stay too, lady.

KENT: Why should she?

DOC: Well, I mean we'll need somebody to mix up some jasmine tea with honey, and——

KENT: Sonny can do that.

SONNY: It needs a woman.

SALEM: Look. Kent's all right now, so why don't the two of you go back and leave me with him alone.

SONNY: You're no doctor.

DOC: Right. Your husband should get some rest now and special tea. Only a doctor with many years experience and——

SALEM: Just what is your experience?

SONNY: Don't talk to Pa like that.

SALEM: And what's this business about cutting wires.

DOC: We never cut your wires, lady.

(KENT *advances on* DOC *as* DOC *backs up.*)

KENT: I thought you said before that you cut our wires.

DOC: Naw. Never did.

KENT: I was under the impression we were juiceless here. Out of touch. No way of reaching the outside.

DOC: Try it then. Pick up the phone and try it.

KENT: Try it, Salem.

(SALEM *goes to the phone and picks up the receiver, as* KENT
backs DOC *around the stage.* SONNY *looks on.*)

DOC: You could call Berlin if you wanted.

KENT: Why would we call Berlin if we wanted?

SALEM: No juice. (*She hangs up.*)

DOC: Now that's downright silly. Sonny, you give it a try.

KENT: Don't move, Sonny, or I'll gun you down.

(SONNY *freezes.*)

DOC: Now go ahead, son. I have a gun. He don't. I'm the one
that's armed. Go on now. Let's settle this once and for all.

KENT: Don't make a move.

DOC: You got a lot a' gall, bucko. Just 'cause you're feelin'
your oats and all, now that you're cured. You're forgettin'
pretty fast who got ya' out a' your dilemma. Remember?
Your old Doc got ya' out a' what looked to me like
suicide. Plain and simple.

(SONNY *stays frozen.*)

SALEM: Don't say that. Kent, let's just leave.

KENT: He'll die if he makes a move.

DOC: Now that's pushin' it right to the edge, mister. You gotta
have a full house to be callin' bluffs like that.

(KENT *draws an imaginary pistol and points it at* DOC, *as he
moves him around the stage faster.* SONNY *stays frozen.*)

KENT: It's been proven that the wires are cut. Salem proved it.

DOC: Now, Sonny, you just go and give it a check, and then we
can leave. Sonny! (*He stays frozen.*)

SALEM: Kent, let him check the phone if he wants. Then we'll go.

DOC: Who are you foolin' with a finger. I ain't from Egypt, ya'
know.

SALEM: Look, I'll phone the operator and show you both.

(*She moves toward the phone and freezes when* DOC *speaks.*)

DOC: Don't make a move!

(*He draws his pistol and aims it at* KENT. *Now* DOC *begins
backing* KENT *around the stage.* KENT *keeps his finger
pointed at* DOC. SALEM *and* SONNY *remain frozen in their
places.*)

KENT: Now why in the world—I ask myself why in the world
would a doctor from a respectable clinic want to disconnect
the phone of a dying man. A man he's supposed to cure.
A man who's prepared to pay him two suitcases full of
money in exchange for his good health. I ask myself why
and come up with only one answer.

DOC: Now what would that be?

KENT: That this doctor is up to no good. That this doctor, in
cahoots with his fishy son, is planning to perform some
strange experiment on this dying man that he don't want
to leak out to the outside world. So if this experiment fails
no one will be the wiser, and the only one to have lost
anything will be the dying man who's dying anyway.
(They change directions again with KENT *advancing and* DOC
retreating.)

DOC: And I ask myself something too. I ask myself why this
dying man who's got nothing to lose but his life accuses
the one and only person who could possibly save it of such
a silly thing as cutting the wires to his telephone. I ask
myself that and come up with only one answer.

KENT: Yes?

DOC: That this dying man isn't dying at all. That this here man
is aching all over for only one thing. And he cunningly
puts the idea into the mind of the doctor, and the doctor
then acts it out. The doctor performs the experiment with
his faithful son at his side and transforms the dying man
into a thing of beauty.

KENT: How?
*(*DOC *advances on* KENT.*)*

DOC: By beginning slow. From the hair down. Piece by piece.
Peeling the scalp away neatly. Carving out the
stickiness and placing cool summer breezes inside. In
place of the hair goes a grassy field with a few dandelions
falling toward the back.

KENT: And the eyes?

DOC: Wet spongy moss covers each one and opens into long
tunnel caves that go like spirals to the back where the light
pours in. The nose swoops down and has crows and

chickadees roosting all day on its tip. The doctor's scalpel moves quickly over the mouth.

(KENT *advances on* DOC.)

KENT: Oh no. The mouth hangs in strips for lips that droop all the way down to the chin. And underneath are thick round teeth with edges sharper than diamonds, so they flash at night when he's eating. The flashing warn everything living within twenty miles, and they stay inside until morning comes.

DOC: The chin——

KENT: I told you! You can't see the chin because of the lips. They hang down. And so does the hair. Long sheets of black hair that hang down past its waist and rustle like paper when it runs.

(DOC *advances on* KENT.)

DOC: Doc and his faithful son stay up through the night thinking of shoulders and arms and a chest for the beast.

(SONNY *makes a sudden move for the phone but freezes when* KENT *yells.*)

KENT: Hold it! I'll blow you to bits!

DOC: At 3 a.m., they get down to work. Moving fast and patiently over the torso. The arms dangle down past its hair and gently flow into beautiful womanly hands that look like they've never been outside of goatskin gloves until this very moment.

KENT: When it jerks up its head and bursts from the leather strap across its thin chest.

DOC: No!

(KENT *advances on* DOC.)

KENT: But then it's too late. The moment has come for its birth, and nothing can stop it from coming.

(KENT *stalks* DOC *with his finger pointed at him: he manipulates* DOC *all over the stage while the others stay frozen in place.*)

DOC: Not yet! There's the legs and the feet left to do!

KENT: It opens its arms and its mouth and tests everything out. It feels how the juices drain from its brain, down through the nose and into the mouth where it tastes like honey. He licks. He kicks off the sheets. He rolls off the edge of the stainless steel table that rolls on its tiny rubber wheels straight for the wall.

DOC: You can't start before——

KENT: The fall from the table to the floor starts other juices going. He feels the stream of fluid pulling him off the ground and on to his feet.

DOC: He can't even walk! He doesn't have feet!

(KENT *changes his finger from a gun to a knife and begins making quick lunges toward* DOC, *who jumps back.*)

KENT: He finds the fluid pounds through his legs and his waist. It catches hold and loosens up. It draws back and snaps out like a snake. He moves across the room in two steps and flattens out against the wall. He disappears and becomes the wall. He reappears on the opposite wall. He clings to the floor and slithers along. Underneath cages of rats and rabbits and monkeys and squirrels. He becomes a mouse and changes into a cobra and then back on the floor. Then on to the roof.

DOC: Stop it!

(DOC *fires the pistol.* KENT *keeps advancing: his gestures and movements become wildly extravagant, like an African dance.* DOC *retreats to every corner of the room, running away, while* SALEM *and* SONNY *stay frozen.*)

KENT: Then jumping from roof to roof with his paper hair flying behind and his lips curling back from the wind and tasting the juice that's pouring down from his nose and his ears.
(DOC *fires again.*)
He zigzags sharply around TV antennas and his ears catch the sound of the dogs panting as they rush up the steps to the top of the roof. He can hear barking and screaming and whistles. Beams of white light cut through the night and follow his trail. Sirens sound through the streets.
(DOC *fires.*)
He keeps jumping space after space and roof after roof. And each jump he makes he looks down right in mid-air between the roof he left behind and the roof he's jumping to. He looks down and he sees a miniature world where things move like bedbugs and ticks. And then he looks up

and he sees miniature lights that flick on and off.
(KENT *leaps off the stage and on to the ramp: he runs up the ramp and behind the audience, where he speaks.* DOC *intercedes with his lines from the stage.*)

DOC:

Now come back down here and stop playin' around!

I ain't playin' around any more!

I'll walk right out on ya' boy!

I'd just a' soon let ya' rot away!

There ain't nothin' keeping me here.

Now ya' gotta be fair about this!

KENT:

The Doctor is torn by desires that cut through his brain as he leads the hysterical mob on the trail of the beast he once loved.

Now it must be destroyed. If he could somehow get to the beast ahead of the mob. Trap it somehow in a quiet place between smooth wet boulders, and talk to it calmly.

Perhaps even stroke its long hair and wipe off its chin. To find some way of telling the beast that the mob will calm down if *he* only does.

The Doctor makes a dash away from the mob and ducks into a dark stand of sycamore trees. The mob is confused and frightened without the Doctor. They become enraged and set the forest on fire.

Doc moves away from the flames easily, since he's passed through this section of land many times before on his calls.

DOC:

I done all I could. I diagnosed
the disease. I treated what ails
ya'! I can't do no more! What
more can I do?

KENT:

He finds a narrow stream,
where he usually drinks on his
way back and forth and slowly
submerges under the surface.
He swims along easily and
lets the current propel him
downstream. Moving through
flowing green plants and
yellow goldfish, and surfacing
once in a while to check where
he is.

The monster has a complete
view now, from his perch.

I gotta keep my distance, boy!
A doctor has got to keep a
distance! I mean I can't go
falling asleep on the job!

He sees the stream cutting the
land in half, with one-half on
fire, and the other half dark
and quiet. He's calmer now
and sits on a rock, catching
up with his breath.

Look what would happen if
that were to happen!

The Doctor comes up on to
the shore panting for breath
and clutching at long clumps
of grass.

He drags himself up on dry
land and staggers on through
the night. Afraid if he stops
for a rest that the beast will
be lost forever.

Now the beast begins to even
enjoy being up so high. Above
everything else but the sky
and watching the golden fire

DOC:	KENT:
	move down one side of the stream and consuming everything dark.
(DOC's "look" sequence during this: DOC goes through different gestures that were KENT's in the first Act; running to the bathroom, swaggering, fainting, etc.)	Doc begins to feel lost now in the trees with no living thing around him but leaves that whistle and hum as though sensing the fire's approach. He must find the beast. He begins to think if I were him how would I hide and how would I run? Which way would I go and how would I choose?
I gotta keep strong!	The beast even likes the idea of not having to move. To sit in one place on a smooth shiny rock and just swivel to different positions and face in different directions.
That's my job!	
To keep strong and quick and alert!	
I mean what earthly good would I be to you or to anyone else if I was walkin' around just as sick as my patients? No good at all. Now you can see that as plain as I can. That's why I make a point to keep fit.	Doc bends slowly downward and finds he moves faster with his head pushing him on. He seeks out the shadowy places, always staying upwind and straining his eyes to find a higher place.
That's why I am always in shape.	Gently, the monster pulls the moss flaps back from his eyes and lets the wind fill them up.
	His beautiful hands stroke the smooth rock.

DOC:

Notice that! My eyes are clear! My skin is smooth! My hair is free of lice and ticks! My muscles are well tuned up for any situation! Just watch me! Look at the way I can move if I want! You should trust me, boy! I'll get ya' through! Just let me show ya' the way! You'll have to go with me though! I can't go with you! I'll show ya' how! Step by step. One foot in front of the other foot. Let your arms swing free at the sides. Let the words come.

KENT:

He chuckles at the spits that the fire makes as it reaches the stream and goes out. Doc's feet slip and clutch the shale rock and sand and his hands grasp for vines and stumps and roots and anything strong enough to hoist his aching body up to the top. The beast stretches and yawns and smiles. He misses only one thing: the face of the Doc the way it used to be, looking down and smiling with his big dark eyes and his scalpel in hand.

(DOC *goes to* SONNY *and* SALEM *and shakes them out of their freeze as he continues to talk to* KENT. *Slowly he gets them to move, he points to* KENT *and persuades them to try to bring him back on the stage. They slowly move downstage, like somnambulists. As* DOC *remains on stage talking to* KENT *they move off the stage and on to the ramp toward* KENT. SALEM *and* SONNY *hum, "When Johnny Comes Marching Home Again," as they close in on* KENT.)

DOC:

Yes, sir, ya' won't have no trouble at all if ya' go along with the cure. We'll be unbeatable, the two of us.

KENT:

Doc almost forgets why he's climbing so fast and so hard until he hears shouts from the dark side of the forest at the base of the hill. They've crossed the river and picked up his trail. Doc prises loose a boulder and lets it crash down the side.

DOC:
I'll get ya' one a' them pinto
stallions with a silver saddle
and a golden bit.

And hand tooled Indian boots.
I'll show ya' how to use a
thirty odd six and a forty odd
eight. You don't have to worry
your head about nothin' boy!
We'll walk into each town
like they was puddles a' water
waiting around for a boot to
come by and splash them out
a' their hole. We'll always be
taken care of, you and me.
Always! Just wait and see.

Get him! Grab ahold of his
arms! Get him back down
here! Don't let him get away!

KENT:
His beautiful hands are bleeding from clawing. His feet feel
like they're not even there.

He lunges and pulls toward
the top. He twists in and out
of small thorny bushes. He
squeezes in between cracks
in the rock as bullets ring out
and torches flare in the sides
of his eyes. He uses his mouth
to pull himself up, and his
diamond teeth blind the mob
with their flash. Doc must get
there first and escape with the
beast.

His arms rip from the shoulders and chest, and juices gush
out down his sides. He must
find him there and hide in a
cave. His hair tears and floats
away, flapping in air like an
owl at night looking for mice
in the field far below. He
must meet him alone for one
final time. His teeth drag him
up. Dragging the body along.
Pulling and chomping down
on the earth. Pulling up and
chomping down.

(SALEM *and* SONNY *make a lunge for* KENT, *who grabs on to a
rope and swings over their heads. He lands on the ramp behind*
DOC *and runs straight toward the upstage wall of the set and leaps
right through it, leaving a cut-out silhouette of his body in the
wall. The lights dim out as the other three stare at the wall.*)

The Tooth of Crime

A Play with Music in Two Acts

The play was first performed at the Open Space, London, on 17 July 1972. The cast was as follows:

HOSS	Malcolm Storry
BECKY LOU	Petronella Ford
STAR-MAN	Michael Weller
GALACTIC JACK	Tony Milner
REFEREE	
CHEYENNE	Tony Sibbalt
DOC	John Grillo
CROW	David Schofield

Directed by Charles Marowitz, assisted by Walter Donohue
Designed by Robin Don
Music composed by Sam Shepard, and arranged and played by Blunderpuss

ACT ONE

SCENE: *A bare stage except for an evil-looking black chair with silver studs and a very high back, something like an Egyptian Pharaoh's throne but simple, center stage. In the dark, heavy lurking Rock and Roll starts low and builds as the lights come up. The band should be hidden. The sound should be like 'Heroin' by the Velvet Underground. When the lights are up full,* Hoss *enters in black rocker gear with silver studs and black kid gloves. He holds a microphone. He should look like a mean Rip Torn but a little younger. He takes the stage and sings 'The Way Things Are'. The words of the song should be understood so the band has to back off on volume when he starts singing.*

    'The Way Things Are'
Hoss: You may think every picture you see is a true history
    of the way things used to be or the way things are
    While you're ridin' in your radio or walkin' through
    the late late show ain't it a drag to know you just don't
        know
    you just don't know
    So here's another illusion to add to your confusion
    Of the way things are
    Everybody's doin' time for everybody else's crime
        and
    I can't swim for the waves in the ocean
    All the heroes is dyin' like flies they say it's a sign a'
    the times
    And everybody's walkin' asleep eyes open — eyes open

    So here's another sleep-walkin' dream
    A livin' talkin' show of the way things seem

I used to believe in rhythm and blues
Always wore my blue suede shoes
Now everything I do goes down in doubt

But sometimes in the blackest night I can see a little light
That's the only thing that keeps me rockin' — keeps me rockin'

So here's another fantasy
About the way things seem to be to me.

(He finishes the song and throws down the microphone and yells off stage.)
Beck Lou!
(BECKY comes on in black rock and roll gear. She's very tall and blonde. She holds two black satchels, one in each hand. They should look like old country-doctor bags.)
BECKY: Ready just about.
HOSS: Let's have a look at the gear.
(BECKY sets the bags down on the floor and opens them. She pulls out a black velvet piece of cloth and lays it carefully on the floor then she begins to take out pearl-handled revolvers, pistol, derringers and rifles with scopes, shotguns broken down. All the weapons should look really beautiful and clean. She sets them carefully on the velvet cloth. HOSS picks up the rifles and handles them like a pro, cocking them and looking down the barrel through the scope, checking out the chambers on the pistols and running his hands over them as though they were alive.)
How's the Maserati?
BECKY: Clean. Greased like a bullet. Cheyenne took it up to 180 on the Ventura Freeway then backed her right down. Said she didn't bark once.
HOSS: Good. About time he stopped them quarter-mile orgasms. They were rippin' her up. Gotta let the gas flow in a machine like that. She's Italian. Likes a full-tilt feel.
BECKY: Cheyenne's hungry for long distance now. Couldn't hold him back with nails. Got lead in his gas foot.
HOSS: These look nice and blue. Did the Jeweler check 'em out?

BECKY: Yeah, Hoss. Everything's taken care of.

HOSS: Good. Now we can boogie.

BECKY: What's the moon chart say?

HOSS: Don't ask me! I hired a fucking star-man. A gazer. What the fuck's he been doin' up there.

BECKY: I don't know. Last I knew it was the next first quarter moon. That's when he said things'd be right.

HOSS: Get that fucker down here! I wanna see him. I gave him thirteen grand to get this chart in line. Tell him to get his ass down here!

BECKY: O.K., O.K.

(She exits, HOSS caresses the guns.)

HOSS: That fuckin' Scorpion's gonna crawl if this gets turned around now. Now is right. I can feel it's right. I need the points! Can't they see that! I'm winning in three fucking States! I'm controlling more borders than any a' them punk Markers. The El Camino Boys. Bunch a' fuckin' punks. GET THAT FUCKER DOWN HERE!!!

(STAR-MAN enters with BECKY. He's dressed in silver but shouldn't look like Star Trek, more contemporary silver.)

O.K., slick face, what's the scoop. Can we move now?

STAR-MAN: Pretty risky, Hoss.

HOSS: I knew it! I knew it! You fuckin' creep! Every time we get hot to trot you throw on the ice water. Whatsa matter now.

STAR-MAN: Venus is entering Scorpio.

HOSS: I don't give a shit if it's entering Brigitte Bardot. I'm ready for a kill!

STAR-MAN: You'll blow it.

HOSS: I'll blow it. What do you know. I've always moved on a sixth sense. I don't need you, meatball.

BECKY: Hoss, you never went against the charts before.

HOSS: Fuck before. This time I feel it. I can smell blood. It's right. The time is right! I'm fallin' behind. Maybe you don't understand that.

STAR-MAN: Not true, Hoss. The El Caminos are about six points off the pace. Mojo Rootforce is the only one close enough to even worry about.

HOSS: Mojo? That fruit? What'd he knock over?

STAR-MAN: Vegas, Hoss. He rolled the big one.

HOSS: Vegas! He can't take Vegas, that's my mark! That's against the code!

STAR-MAN: He took it.

HOSS: I don't believe it.

BECKY: We picked it up on the bleeper.

HOSS: When? How come I'm the last to find out?

STAR-MAN: We thought it'd rattle you too much.

HOSS: When did it happen!

STAR-MAN: This morning from what the teleprompters read.

HOSS: I'm gonna get that chump. I'm gonna have him. He can't do that. He knew Vegas was on my ticket. He's trying to shake me. He thinks I'll just jump borders and try suburban shots. Well he's fuckin' crazy. I'm gonna roll him good.

BECKY: You can't go against the code, Hoss. Once a Marker strikes and sets up colors, that's his turf. You can't strike claimed turf. They'll throw you out of the game.

HOSS: *He* did it! He took my mark. It was on my ticket goddamnit!

STAR-MAN: He can just claim his wave system blew and he didn't find out till too late.

HOSS: Well he's gonna find out now. I'll get a fleet together and wipe him out.

BECKY: But, Hoss, you'll be forced to change class. You won't have solo rights no more. You'll be a gang man. A punk.

HOSS: I don't care. I want that fuckin' gold record and nobody's gonna stop me. Nobody!

STAR-MAN: You gotta hold steady, Hoss. This is a tender time. The wrong move'll throw you back a year or more. You can't afford that now. The charts are moving too fast. Every week there's a new star. You don't wanna be a flybynight mug in the crowd. You want something durable, something lasting. How're you gonna cop an immortal shot if you give up soloing and go into a gang war. They'll rip you up in a night. Sure you'll have a few moments of global glow, maybe even an interplanetary flash. But it won't last, Hoss, it won't last.

BECKY: He's right, Hoss.

HOSS: O.K., O.K. I'm just gettin' hungry that's all. I need a kill. I haven't had a kill for months now. You know what that's like. I gotta kill. It's my whole life. If I don't kill I get crazy. I start eating away at myself. It's not good. I was born to kill.

STAR-MAN: Nobody knows that better than us, Hoss. But you gotta listen to management. That's what we're here for. To advise and direct. Without us you'd be just like a mad dog again. Can't you remember what that was like.

HOSS: Yeah, yeah! Go away now. Go on! I wanna be alone with Becky.

STAR-MAN: O.K. Just try and take it easy. I know you were wired for a big kill but your time is coming. Don't forget that.

HOSS: Yeah, all right. Beat it!

(STAR-MAN *exits leaving* HOSS *alone with* BECKY. *He looks around the stage dejected. He kicks at the guns and pulls off his gloves.*)

I'm too old fashioned. That's it. Gotta kick out the scruples. Go against the code. That's what they used to do. The big ones. Dylan, Jagger, Townsend. All them cats broke codes. Time can't change that.

BECKY: But they were playin' pussy, Hoss. They weren't killers ... You're a killer, man. You're in the big time.

HOSS: So were they. My Pa told me what it was like. They were killers in their day too. Cold killers.

BECKY: Come on. You're talkin' treason against the game. You could get the slammer for less than that.

HOSS: Fuck 'em. I know my power. I can go on Gypsy Kill and still gain status. There's a whole underground movement going on. There's a lot of Gypsy Markers comin' up.

BECKY: Why do you wanna throw everything away. You were always suicidal like that. Right from the start.

HOSS: It's part of my nature.

BECKY: That's what we saved you from, your nature. Maybe you forgot that. When we first landed you, you were a complete beast of nature. A sideways killer. Then we molded and shaped you and sharpened you down to perfection because we saw in you a true genius killer. A killer to end them all. A killer's killer.

HOSS: Aw fuck off. I don't believe that shit no more. That stuff is for schoolies. Sure I'm good. I might even be great but I ain't no genius, Genius is something outside the game. The game can't contain a true genius. It's too small. The next genius is gonna be a Gypsy Killer. I can feel it. I know it's goin' down right now. We don't have the whole picture. We're too successful ... We're insulated from what's really happening by our own fame.

BECKY: You're really trying to self-destruct aren't you? Whatsa matter, you can't take fame no more? You can't hold down the pressure circuits? Maybe you need a good lay or two.

HOSS: Your ass. I can handle the image like a fuckin' jockey. It's just that I don't trust the race no more. I dropped the blinkers.

BECKY: You're not gettin' buck fever are ya'?

HOSS: Get outa' here!

BECKY: Come on. Put it in fourth for a while, Hoss. Cruise it. You can afford to take it easy.

HOSS: GET THE FUCK OUTA' HERE!!!

BECKY: O.K., O.K. I'm your friend. Remember?

HOSS: Yeah, sure.

BECKY: I am. You're in a tough racket. The toughest. But now ain't the time to crack. You're knockin' at the door, Hoss. You gotta hold on. Once you get the gold then you can back off. But not now.

HOSS: I'm not backin' off. I'm just havin' a doubt dose.

BECKY: Maybe I should call a D.J. One a' the big ones. Then you could sit down with him and he could lay the charts out right in front of you. Show you exactly where you stand.

HOSS: That's a good idea. Good. Go get one. Get Galactic Jack and his Railroad Track. Tell him to bring his latest charts. Go on!

BECKY: O.K. I'll be back.

(She exits. HOSS stalks around the stage building up his confidence.)

HOSS: She's right! She's right goddamnit! I'm so fucking close. Knockin' at the door. I can't chicken out of it now. This is my last chance. I'm gettin' old. I can't do a Lee Marvin in the late sixties. I can't pull that number off. I've stomped

too many heads. I'm past shitkicker class now. Past the
rumble. I'm in the big time. Really big. It's now or never.
Come on, Hoss, be a killer, man. Be a killer!
(Music starts. He sings 'Cold Killer'.)
'Cold Killer'
I'm a cold killer Mama — I got blood on my jeans
I got a Scorpion star hangin' over me
I got snakes in my pockets and a razor in my boot
You better watch it don't get you — It's faster'n you can
    shoot
I got the fastest action in East L.A.
I got the fastest action in San Berdoo
And if you don't believe it lemme shoot it to you

Now watch me slide into power glide — supercharged
    down the line
There ain't no way for you to hide from the killer's eye
My silver studs, my black kid gloves make you cry inside
But there ain't no way for you to hide from the killer's eye

I'm a cold killer Mama — and I've earned my tattoo
I got a Pachooko cross hangin' over you
I got whiplash magic and a rattlesnake tongue
My John the Conqueroot says I'm the cold gun

Now watch me slide into power-glide — supercharged down
the line
There ain't no way for you to hide from the killer's eye
My silver studs, my black kid gloves make you cry inside
But there ain't no way for you to hide from the killer's eye.

(The song ends. BECKY *enters with* GALACTIC JACK, *the disc
jockey. He's white and dressed like a 42nd Street pimp, pink
shirt, black tie, black patent leather shoes, white panama
straw hat and a flash suit. He talks like Wolfman Jack and
carries a bundle of huge charts.)*
Ah! The man. Galactic Jack and his Railroad Track.
GALACTIC JACK: That's me, Jim. Heavy duty and on the whim.
    Back flappin', side trackin', finger poppin', reelin' rockin'
    with the tips on the picks in the great killer race. All tricks,

no sale, no avail. It's in the can and on the lam. Grease it, daddyo!

(He holds out his hand palm up for HOSS *to give him five.* HOSS *holds back.)*

HOSS: Back down, Jack. Just give it to me straight. Am I risin' or fallin'.

GALACTIC JACK: A shootin' star, baby, High flyin' and no jivin'. You is off to number nine.

HOSS: Show me what you got. Just lay it out on the floor.

BECKY: Shall I get ya'll some drinks?

HOSS: Yeah. Tequila Gold. What do you take, Jack?

GALACTIC JACK: Not me, baby. I'm runnin' reds all down the spine. Feelin' fine and mixin's a crime.

BECKY: Right.

(She exits. JACK *lays his chart on the floor.* HOSS *and* JACK *crouch down to get a close inspection.)*

GALACTIC JACK: O.K. Here's the stand on the national band. The game's clean now. Solo is the word. Gang war is takin' a back seat. The Low Riders are outa' the picture and you is in, Jim. In like a stone winner.

HOSS: Don't hype it up, Jack. Just show me how it's movin'. I was ready to take Nevada clean and that meathead Mojo Rootforce rolled Vegas.

GALACTIC JACK: Yeah I heard that. Supposed to be on your ticket too. Bad news.

HOSS: He can't get away with that can he?

GALACTIC JACK: I can't dope them sheets, Hoss. You'll have to consult a Ref for the rules or go straight to the Keepers.

HOSS: I can't go to the game Keepers. They'll ask for an itinerary and question past kills. I can't afford a penalty now. I need every point.

GALACTIC JACK: Well lookee here. There's movement all around but no numero uno. That's what they're backin' their chips on you for, boy. The bookies got you two to one.

HOSS: That close?

GALACTIC JACK: All of 'em runnin' it down to you. There's Little Willard from the East in his formula Lotus. Fast machine. Doin' O.K. with a stainless steel Baretta.

HOSS: Willard's solo now?

GALACTIC JACK: Yeah but no threat. Just a front runner. Lots a'
early speed but can't go the distance. Here's one outa Tupelo
called Studie Willcock. Drivin' a hot Merc, dual cams,
Chrysler through and through. Fast but not deadly. He's
offed four in a week and almost had Arkansas wrapped up
but he's fadin' fast. You're it, Jim. You is the coldest on the
circuit.

HOSS: What about this mark? *(pointing at the charts)*

GALACTIC JACK: Oh yeah, that's Grease Jam. Got a supercharged Mini Cooper. Takes the corners. Tried a hit on St.
Paul and almost had Minnesota to its knees when he blew a
head gasket. Some say he's even been offed by the El
Caminos.

HOSS: Those guys are pressin' it pretty hard. They're gonna get
blown off sooner or later.

GALACTIC JACK: No doubt. No need to pout. The course is clear.
Maybe a few Gypsy Killers comin' into the picture but
nothin' to fret your set.

HOSS: Gypsies? Where? I knew it. I got a feeling.

GALACTIC JACK: Just some side bets. They go anonymous 'cause
a' the code. One slip and they is pissed. You can dig it.
They's playin' with the king fire.

HOSS: But they got a following right? They're growing in the
polls?

GALACTIC JACK: Hard to suss it yet, man. Some polls don't even
mention their kills for fear of the Keepers comin' down on
'em. I could maybe sound some flies for ya'. See if I could
whiff some sniff on that action.

HOSS: Yeah, do.

GALACTIC JACK: What's the keen to the Gypsy scene. These boys
are losin' to the cruisin' baby.

HOSS: They've got time on their side. Can't you see that. The
youth's goin' to 'em. The kids are flocking to Gypsy Kills.
It's a market opening up, Jack. I got a feeling. I know
they're on their way in and we're going out. We're gettin'
old, Jack.

GALACTIC JACK: You just got the buggered blues, man. You been
talkin' to the wrong visions. You gotta get a head set. Put

yer ears on straight. Zoot yerself down, boy. These Gypsies is committin' suicide. We got the power. We got the game. If the Keepers whimsy it all they do is scratch 'em out. Simple. They're losers, man. The bookies don't even look past their left shoulder at a Gypsy mark. They won't last, man. Believe me.

HOSS: I don't know. There's power there. Full blown.

GALACTIC JACK: They don't know the ropes, man. Rules is out. They're into slaughter straight off. Not a clean kill in the bunch.

HOSS: But they got balls. They're on their own.

GALACTIC JACK: So are you. Solo's the payolo.

HOSS: But I'm inside and they're out. They could unseat us all.

GALACTIC JACK: Not a King. The crown sticks where it fits and right now it looks about your size.

HOSS: What if they turned the game against us. What if they started marking us!

GALACTIC JACK: That's revolution, man.

HOSS: You hit it.

GALACTIC JACK: Old time shuffle. Don't stand a chance at this dance.

HOSS: But that's how we started ain't it. We went up against the Dudes. Wiped 'em out.

GALACTIC JACK: The Dudes weren't pros, man. You gotta see where you stand. I do believe you is tastin' fear. Runnin' scared. These Gypsies is just muck-rakers. Second hand, one night stand. They ain't worth shit on shinola in your league. Dig yourself on the flip side. You're number one with a bullet and you ain't even got the needle in the groove.

HOSS: We'll see. Somethin's goin' down big out there. The shit's gonna hit the fan before we can get to the bank.

GALACTIC JACK: Take a deep knee bend, Hoss. It's just the pre-victory shakes. Tomorrow you'll have the gold in your hand. The bigee. Don't be shy, I tell no lie. Catch ya' on the re-bop. Say bye and keep the slide greased down.

HOSS: Yeah. Thanks.

(JACK *collects his chart and exits.* HOSS *paces and talks to himself.*)

(to himself) Come on, come on. Confidence, man.

Confidence. Don't go on the skids now. Keep it together. Tighten down. Talk it out. Quit jumpin' at shadows. They got you goose bumped and they ain't even present. Put yourself in their place. They got nothin'.You got it all. All the chips. Come on dice! Come on dice! That's it. Roll 'em sweet. The sweet machine. Candy in the gas tank. Floor it. Now you got the wheel. Take it. Take it!

(BECKY *enters with the drink.* HOSS *catches himself.*)

BECKY: What happened to Jack?

HOSS: We ran the session.

BECKY: Here's your drink.

HOSS: Thanks. Listen, Becky, is Cheyenne ready to roll?

BECKY: Yeah. He's hot. Why?

HOSS: Maybe we could just do a cruise. No action. Just some scouting. I'm really feelin' cooped up in here. This place is drivin' me nuts.

BECKY: Too dangerous, Hoss. We just got word that Eyes sussed somebody's marked you.

HOSS: What! Marked *me*? Who?

BECKY: One a' the Gypsies.

HOSS: It's all comin' down like I said. I must be top gun then.

BECKY: That's it.

HOSS: They gotta be fools, man. A Gypsy's marked *me*?

BECKY: That's the word from Eyes.

HOSS: Where is he?

BECKY: Vegas.

HOSS: Vegas? Oh now I get it. Mojo. He's hired a Gypsy to off me clean. That's it. That fuckin' chicken shit. I'm gonna blast him good. Doesn't have the balls to come down to me. Gotta hire a Gypsy.

BECKY: Might be just a renegade solo, Hoss. They're all lookin' to put you under. You're the main trigger. The word's out.

HOSS: Don't you get it? The Rootforce is slip-streamin' my time. Takin' my marks and hirin' amateurs to rub me out. It's a gang shot. They're workin' doubles. I gotta team up now. It's down to that. I gotta get ahold a' Little Willard. Get him on the line.

BECKY: Hoss, don't fly off, man. You're safe here.

HOSS: Safe! Safe and amputated from the neck down! I'm a
Marker man, not a desk clerk. Get fucking Willard to the
phone! And tell Cheyenne to come in here!
(BECKY exits)
O.K. Now the picture brightens. I can play for high stakes
now. I can draw to the straight, outside or in. I'm ready to
take on any a' these flash heads. Vegas is mine, man. It
belongs in my pocket. The West is mine. I could even take
on the Keepers. That's it. I'll live outside the fucking law
altogether. Outside the whole shot. That's it. Why didn't I
think a' that before!
*(CHEYENNE enters in green velvet with silver boots and
racing gloves.)*
CHEYENNE: You want me, Hoss?
HOSS: Yeah! Yeah I want you! You're my main man.
(He gives CHEYENNE a bear hug.)
Listen, Cheyenne, we done a lotta' marks in our time.
Right?
CHEYENNE: Yeah.
HOSS: Good clean kills. Honest kills. But now the times are
changin'. The race is deadly. Mojo Rootforce is movin' in on
turf marks and tryin' to put me out with a Gypsy.
CHEYENNE: A Gypsy?
HOSS: Yeah.
CHEYENNE: They can't do that. It's against the code.
HOSS: Fuck the code. Nobody's playin' by the rules no more. We
been suckers to the code for too long now. Now we move
outside. You remember Little Willard?
CHEYENNE: East Coast. Drove a Galaxie. Into Remington over
and unders.
HOSS: Yeah. He's changed his style now. Got himself a Lotus
Formula 2 and a Baretta.
CHEYENNE: Sounds mean.
HOSS: He is man. And I trust him. He was right with me when
we took off the Dudes. Becky's on the phone to him now.
He's our man. Just him and us.
CHEYENNE: But Rootforce has probably got Vegas locked up,
Hoss. It's gonna be hard penetration.

HOSS: We rolled Phoenix didn't we?

CHEYENNE: Yeah.

HOSS: Tucson?

CHEYENNE: Yeah.

HOSS: San Berdoo?

CHEYENNE: Yeah.

HOSS: So Vegas ain't no Fort Knox.

CHEYENNE: So it's back to the rumble?

HOSS: Temporary. Just temporary. We can't sit back and let the good times roll when the game's breakin' down.

CHEYENNE: I don't know. I love the game, Hoss. I ain't hot to go back to gang war.

HOSS: We got to now! Otherwise we're down the tubes.

CHEYENNE: What about the Keepers?

HOSS: Fuck them too. We'll take 'em all on.

CHEYENNE: The critics won't like it.

HOSS: The critics! They're outside, man. They don't know what's goin' on.

CHEYENNE: What about our reputation. We worked hard to get where we are. I'm not ready to throw that away. I want a taste a' that gold.

HOSS: I'm surrounded by ass holes! Can't you see what's happened to us. We ain't Markers no more. We ain't even Rockers. We're punk chumps cowering under the Keepers and the Refs and the critics and the public eye. We ain't free no more! Goddamnit! We ain't flyin' in the eye of contempt. We've become respectable and safe. Soft, mushy chewable ass lickers. What's happened to our killer heart. What's happened to our blind fucking courage! Cheyenne, we ain't got much time, man. We were warriors once.

CHEYENNE: That was a long time ago.

HOSS: Then you're backing down?

CHEYENNE: No. I'm just playin' the game.

(CHEYENNE exits)

HOSS: God! Goddamnit! This is gettin' weird now. Solo ain't the word for it. It's gettin' lonely as an ocean in here. My driver's gone against me and my time's runnin' thin. Little Willard's my last chance. Him and me. He's runnin' without

a driver, so can I. The two of us. Just the two of us. That's
enough against the Rootforce. He's East Coast though.
Maybe he don't know the Western ropes. He could learn it.
We'll cruise the action. He'll pick up the streets. Cheyenne
knows the West though. Born and raised like me. Backyard
schoolin'. Goddamn! Why's he have to go soft now! Why
now!

(BECKY *enters*)

You get Willard?

BECKY: No.

HOSS: How come! I need him bad. Keep tryin'!!

BECKY: He's dead, Hoss. Shot himself in the mouth.

HOSS: Who told you?

BECKY: His Rep. They just found him in New Haven slumped
over an intersection. They say his car was still runnin'.

HOSS: Why'd he go and do that? He was in the top ten and risin'.

BECKY: Couldn't take it I guess. Too vulnerable. They found a
pound of Meth in the back seat.

HOSS: Becky, I'm marked. What the fuck am I gonna do? I can't
just sit here and wait for him to come.

BECKY: Least you'll know he's comin'. If you go out cruisin' he's
liable to strike anywhere, any time. A Gypsy's got the jump
on you that way.

HOSS: What if I busted into Vegas myself? Just me. They'd never
expect somethin' like that. I could take off Mojo and split
before they knew what happened.

BECKY: You're dealin' with a pack now, man. It ain't one against
one no more.

HOSS: Well what am I gonna do!

BECKY: Wait him out. Meet him on a singles match and bounce
him hard. Challenge him.

HOSS: What if he snipes me?

BECKY: We got the watch out. We'll give him the usher routine.
Say that you've been expecting him. That'll challenge his
pride. Then fight him with shivs.

HOSS: Shivs! I ain't used a blade for over ten years. I'm out of
practice.

BECKY: Practise up. I'll get you a set and a dummy.

HOSS: O.K. And call in the Doc. I need a good shot.

BECKY: Good.

(She exits. HOSS *stalks the stage.)*

HOSS: Backed into a fucking box. I can't believe it. Things have changed that much. They don't even apprentice no more. Just mark for the big one. No respect no more. When I was that age I'd sell my leathers to get a crack at a good teacher. I would. And I had some a' the best. There's no sense of tradition in the game no more. There's no game. It's just back to how it was. Rolling night clubs, strip joints. Bustin' up poker games. Zip guns in the junk yard. Rock fights, dirt clods, bustin' windows. Vandals, juvies, West Side Story. Can't they see where they're goin'! Without a code it's just crime. No art involved. No technique, finesse. No sense of mastery. The touch is gone.

*(*BECKY *enters with* DOC *who is dressed in red.* BECKY *has two knives and a dummy which she sets up center stage right.* HOSS *sits in his chair.* DOC *has a syringe and a vial of dope and a rubber surgical hose.* HOSS *rolls his sleeve up and* DOC *goes about shooting him up.)*

Oh, Doc, it's good to see ya'. I'm in need. I'm under the gun, Doc.

DOC: Yeah. Things are tough now. This'll cool you out.

HOSS: Good. Doc, what do you think about Gypsy Kills. Do you think it's ethical?

DOC: Haven't thought too much about it actually. I suppose it was bound to happen. Once I remember this early Gypsy. I guess you'd call him a Gypsy now but at the time he was just a hard luck fella name a' Doc Carter. Little got to be known of the man on account a' the fact that he was ridin' a certain William F. Cody's shirttail all through the West, and, for that matter, half around the planet. Anyhow, ole Doc came to be known as the 'Spirit Gun of the West' and a well-deserved title it was, too. That boy could shoot the hump off a buffalo on the backside of a nickel at a hundred paces. To this very day his saddle is settin' in some musty ole Wyoming museum decorated with a hundred silver coins. Each one shot through and through with his Colt .45.

And all surroundin' this saddle is pictures tall as a man of
this William F. Cody fella pallin' it up with the Indians. Ole
Doc never got out from behind the shadow a' that Cody. But
I suppose nowadays he'd just take over the whole show.
Don't rightly know what made me think a' that. Just
popped into my mind.

HOSS: Yeah. It's just funny finding myself on the other side.

BECKY: It ain't revolution, man. This Gypsy's a hired trigger
from Mojo. He ain't a martyr.

HOSS: But he works outside the code.

BECKY: Fuck it. All you gotta worry about is gettin' him before
he gets you.

HOSS: You were one of the ones who taught me the code. Now
you can throw it away like that.

BECKY: It's back down to survival, Hoss. Temporary suspension.
That's all.

HOSS: I don't think so. I think the whole system's gettin' shot to
shit. I think the code's going down the tubes. These are
gonna be the last days of honor. I can see it comin'.

DOC: There. That oughta' do you for a while.

HOSS: Thanks, Doc.

DOC: If you need any crystal later just call me down.

HOSS: Thanks, man.

(DOC exits)

BECKY: You wanna try these out?

*(She offers the knives to HOSS. He goes limp and relaxed in
the chair.)*

HOSS: Not now. Just come and sit with me for a while.

(BECKY sits at his feet. He strokes her hair.)

Becky?

BECKY: Yeah?

HOSS: You remember the El Monte Legion Stadium?

BECKY: Yeah?

HOSS: Ripple Wine?

BECKY: Yeah.

HOSS: The Coasters?

BECKY *(she sings a snatch)*: 'Take out the papers and the trash
or you don't get no spendin' cash.'

HOSS *(sings)*: 'Just tell your hoodlum friend outside. You ain't
    got time to take a ride.'
BECKY: 'Yackety yack.'
HOSS: 'Don't talk back.'
    (They laugh. HOSS *stops himself.)*
    Don't let me go too soft.
BECKY: Why not. You've earned it.
HOSS: Earned it? I ain't earned nothin'. Everything just
    happened. Just fell like cards. I never made a choice.
BECKY: But you're here now. A hero. All those losers out there
    barkin' at the moon.
HOSS: But where am I goin'? The future's just like the past.
BECKY: You gotta believe, Hoss.
HOSS: In what?
BECKY: Power. That's all there is. The power of the machine.
    The killer Machine. That's what you live and die for. That's
    what you wake up for. Every breath you take you breathe
    the power. You live the power. You are the power.
HOSS: Then why do I feel so weak!
BECKY: The knife's gotta be pulled out before you can stab
    again. The gun's gotta be cocked. The energy's gotta be
    stored. You're just gettin' a trickle charge now. The
    ignition's gotta turn yet.
HOSS: Yeah. It's just hard to wait.
BECKY: It's harder for movers. You're a mover, Hoss. Some
    people, all they do is wait.
HOSS: Maybe I should take a ramble.
BECKY: Where to?
HOSS: Anywhere. Just to get out for a while.
BECKY: You carry your gun wherever you go.
HOSS: Listen, maybe I should go on the lam.
BECKY: Are you crazy?
HOSS: No, I'm serious. I'm gettin' too old for this. I need some
    peace.
BECKY: Do you know what it's like out there, outside the game?
    You wouldn't recognize it.
HOSS: What about New York? Second Avenue.
BECKY: What Second Avenue? There ain't no Second Avenue.

They're all zoned out. You wouldn't stand a snowball's chance in hell of makin' it outside the game. You're too professional. It'd be like keepin' a wild animal as a pet then turnin' him back loose again. You couldn't cope, Hoss.

HOSS: I did it once. I was good on the streets. I was a true hustler.

BECKY: The streets are controlled by the packs. They got it locked up. The packs are controlled by the gangs. The gangs and the Low Riders. They're controlled by cross syndicates. The next step is the Keepers.

HOSS: What about the country. Ain't there any farmers left, ranchers, cowboys, open space? Nobody just livin' their life.

BECKY: You ain't playin' with a full deck, Hoss. All that's gone. That's old time boogie. The only way to be an individual is in the game. You're it. You're on top. You're free.

HOSS: What free! How free! I'm tearin' myself inside out from this fuckin' sport. That's free? That's being alive? Fuck it. I just wanna have some fun. I wanna be a fuck off again. I don't wanna compete no more.

BECKY: And what about the kill? You don't need that?

HOSS: I don't know. Maybe not. Maybe I could live without it.

BECKY: You're talkin' loser now, baby.

HOSS: Maybe so. Maybe I am a loser. Maybe we're all fuckin' losers. I don't care no more.

BECKY: What about the gold record. You don't need that?

HOSS: I don't know! I just wanna back off for a while. I can't think straight. I need a change. A vacation or something.

BECKY: Maybe so. I heard about a place, an island where they don't play the game. Everybody's on downers all day.

HOSS: That sounds good. What about that. Maybe you could find out for me. All I need is a week or two. Just to rest and think things out.

BECKY: I'll see what I can do.

HOSS: Jesus. How'd I get like this?

BECKY: It'll pass.

HOSS: Sing me a song or somethin' would ya? Somethin' to cool me off.

BECKY: O.K.

(She sings)
'Becky's Song'
Lemme take you for a ride down the road
Lean back in the tuck and roll
The radio's broken and I got no beer
But I can ease your load

> Listen to the song that the V-8 sings
> Watch the rhythm of the line
> Isn't it some magic that the night-time brings
> Ain't the highway fine

Tell me where ya' wanna go just take yer pick
All I'm really doin' is cruisin'
Take ya' down to Baton Rouge — New Orleans
Pick us up a Louisiana trick

> Listen to the song that the V-8 sings
> Watch the rhythm of the line
> Isn't it some magic that the night-time brings
> Ain't the highway fine

You could tell me stories of your yesterdays
I could break out a few a' mine
Roll down the window and kiss the wind
Anyway ya' want to ease the time

> Listen to the song that the V-8 sings
> Watch the rhythm of the line
> Isn't it some magic that the night-time brings
> Ain't the highway fine

(The song ends and CHEYENNE *enters.)*

CHEYENNE: Say, Hoss. We just got tapped that the Gypsy's made it through zone five. He's headed this way.

HOSS: Already? What's he drivin'?

CHEYENNE: You won't believe this. A '58 black Impala, fuel injected, bored and stroked, full blown Vet underneath.

HOSS: I'm gonna like this dude. O.K. let him through.

CHEYENNE: All the way?

HOSS: Yeah. Stop him at the moat and sound him on a shiv duel.

CHEYENNE: Shivs? You ain't in shape for blades, Hoss.

HOSS: I can handle it. Walk on.

CHEYENNE: O.K. *(he exits)*

BECKY: Good. He's finally comin'. This'll get ya' back on your feet, Hoss. Your waitin' time is over.

HOSS: Go tell the Doc I want some snow.

BECKY: You want the fit or snort?

HOSS: Snort. Hurry up.

BECKY: Right.

(BECKY exits. HOSS picks up the knives and stalks the dummy. He circles it and talks to the dummy and himself. As he talks he stabs the dummy with sudden violent lunges then backs away again. Blood pours from the dummy onto the floor.)

HOSS: O.K. Gypsy King, where's your true heart. Let's get down now. Let's get down. You talk a good story. You got the true flash but where's yer heart. That's the whole secret. The heart of a Gypsy must be there!

(He stabs at the heart of the dummy then backs off.)

Maybe not. Maybe yer colder than that. Maybe in the neck. Maybe it pumps from the neck down. Maybe there!

(He stabs at the neck then backs off. Blood gushes out.)

All right. All right. A secret's a secret. I can give you that much. But it comes from this end too. I'm your mystery. Figure me. Run me down to your experience. Go ahead. Make a move. Put me in a place. An inch is fatal. Just an inch. The wrong move'll leave you murdered. Come on. Lemme see it. Where's the action? That's not good enough for the back lot even. Here's one!

(He makes a quick move and stabs the dummy in the stomach.)

Now I get it. There ain't no heart to a Gypsy. Just bone. Just blind raging courage. Well that won't do you, boy. That won't take you the full length. Yer up against a pro, kid. A true champion Marker. Yer outclassed before the bell rings. Now you've stepped across the line, boy. No goin' back. Dead on yer feet. *(to himself)* What am I gettin' so wired about? This kid is a punk. It ain't even a contest. He's still

ridin' in the fifties. Beach Boys behind the eye balls. A
blond boy. A fair head. Gang bangs, cheap wine and
bonfires. I could take him in my sleep. I could.
I could —
*(BECKY enters with DOC. DOC has a large sheet of foil with
mounds of cocaine on it. He sets it down on the chair.)*
BECKY: How's it goin'?
HOSS: Something's lacking. I can't seem to get it up like the
other kills. My heart's not in it.
DOC: Have some a' this.
*(He holds out a rolled up hundred dollar bill. HOSS takes it
and goes to the coke.)*
HOSS: Yeah. Maybe that'll help.
(He takes the bill and snorts the coke as he talks.)
You know, I been thinkin'. What if the neutral field state
failed one time. Just once.
BECKY: Like this time for instance?
HOSS: Yeah. Like this time.
BECKY: Then you're a gonner.
DOC: It shouldn't fail, Hoss. You've been trained.
HOSS: I know, but what if an emotional field came through
stronger.
BECKY: Like love or hate?
HOSS: Not that gross, not that simple. Something subtle like the
sound of his voice or a gesture or his timing. Something like
that could throw me off.
BECKY: You're really worried about this Gypsy.
HOSS: Not worried. Intrigued. His style is copping my patterns. I
can feel it already and he's not even here yet. He's got a
presence. Maybe even star quality. His movements have an
aura. Even his short. I mean nobody rides a '58 Impala to
do battle with a star Marker.
BECKY: He's just a fool.
DOC: You gotta stay disengaged, Hoss. The other way is fatal.
HOSS: Maybe not. Maybe there's an opening. A ground wire.
BECKY: For what. He's come to knock you over, man.
HOSS: O.K. but I can play in his key. Find his tuning. Jam a
little before the big kill. I don't have to off him soon's he
walks in the door.

DOC: You'd be better off. He's probably got eyes to work that on you.

HOSS: I don't think so. He's got more class than that. I can feel him coming. We might even be in the same stream. He's got respect.

BECKY: Respect! He's a killer, man.

HOSS: So am I. There's another code in focus here. An outside code. Once I knew this cat in High School who was a Creole. His name was Moose. He was real light skinned and big, curly blond hair, blue eyes. He could pass easy as a jock. Good musician. Tough in football but kinda dumb. Dumb in that way — that people put you down for in High School. Dumb in class. He passed as white until his sister started hangin' around with the black chicks. Then the white kids figured it out. He was black to them even though he looked white. He was a nigger, a coon, a jungle bunny. A Rock Town boy from that day on. We ran together, Moose and me and another cat from Canada who dressed and wore his hair like Elvis. They put him down too because he was too smart. His name was Cruise and he got straight A's without readin' none a' the books. Slept in a garage with his aunt. Built himself a cot right over an old Studebaker. His mother was killed by his father who drove skidders for a lumber company up near Vancouver. Got drunk and busted her in the head with a tire iron. The three of us had a brotherhood, a trust. Something unspoken. Then one day it came to the test. I was sorta' ridin' between 'em. I'd shift my personality from one to the other but they dug me 'cause I'd go crazy drunk all the time. We all went out to Bob's Big Boy in Pasadena to cruise the chicks and this time we got spotted by some jocks from our High School. Our own High School. There were eight of 'em, all crew cut and hot for blood. This was the old days ya' know. So they started in on Cruise 'cause he was the skinniest. Smackin' him around and pushin' him into the car. We was right in the parking lot there. Moose told 'em to ease off but they kept it up. They were really out to choose Moose. He was their mark. They wanted him bad. Girls and dates started gathering around until we was right in the center of a huge crowd a' kids.

Then I saw it. This was a class war. These were rich white kids from Arcadia who got T-birds and deuce coupes for Xmas from Mommy and Daddy. All them cardigan sweaters and chicks with ponytails and pedal pushers and bubble hairdo's. Soon as I saw that I flipped out. I found my strength. I started kickin'shit, man. Hard and fast. Three of 'em went down screamin' and holdin' their balls. Moose and Cruise went right into action. It was like John Wayne, Robert Mitchum and Kirk Douglas all in one movie. Those chumps must a' swung on us three times and that was all she wrote. We had all eight of 'em bleedin' and cryin' for Ma right there in the parking lot at Bob's Big Boy. I'll never forget that. The courage we had. The look in all them rich kids' faces. The way they stepped aside just like they did for 'Big John'. The three of us had a silent pride. We just walked strong, straight into that fuckin' burger palace and ordered three cherry cokes with lemon and a order a' fries.

DOC: Those were the old days.

HOSS: Yeah. Look at me now. Impotent. Can't strike a kill unless the charts are right. Stuck in my image. Stuck in a mansion. Waiting. Waiting for a kid who's probably just like me. Just like I was then. A young blood. And I gotta off him. I gotta roll him or he'll roll me. We're fightin' ourselves. Just like turnin' the blade on ourselves. Suicide, man. Maybe Little Willard was right. Blow your fuckin' brains out. The whole thing's a joke. Stick a gun in your fuckin' mouth and pull the trigger. That's what it's all about. That's what we're doin'. He's my brother and I gotta kill him. He's gotta kill me. Jimmy Dean was right. Drive the fuckin' Spider till it stings ya' to death. Crack up your soul! Jackson Pollock! Duane Allman! Break it open! Pull the trigger! Trigger me! Trigger you! Drive it off the cliff! It's all an open highway. Long and clean and deadly beautiful. Deadly and lonesome as a jukebox.

DOC: Come on, Becky, let's leave him alone.

HOSS: Yeah. Right. Alone. That's me. Alone. That's us. All fucking alone. All of us. So don't go off in your private rooms with pity in mind. Your day is comin'. The mark'll come down to you one way or the other.

BECKY: You better rest, Hoss.

HOSS: Ya' know, you'd be O.K., Becky, if you had a self. So
would I. Something to fall back on in a moment of doubt or
terror or even surprise. Nothin' surprises me no more. I'm
ready to take it all on. The whole shot. The big one. Look at
the Doc. A slave. An educated slave. Look at me. A trained
slave. We're all so pathetic it's downright pathetic. And
confidence is just a hype to keep away the open-ended
shakes. Ain't that the truth, Doc?

DOC: I don't know.

HOSS: Right. Right. 'I don't know' is exactly right. Now beat it,
both of ya' before I rip your fuckin' teeth out a' yer heads!!
GO ON BEAT IT!!!

(BECKY *and* DOC *exit.* HOSS *sits in his chair and stares out in
front of him. He talks to himself sometimes shifting voices
from his own into an older man's.)*

(old) All right, Hoss, this is me talkin'. Yer old Dad. Yer old
fishin' buddy. We used to catch eels side by side down by
the dump. The full moon lit up the stream and the junk. The
rusty chrome flashin' across the marsh. The fireflies
dancin' like a faraway city. They'd swallow the hook all the
way down. You remember that? *(himself)* Yeah. Sure. *(old)*
O.K. You're not so bad off. It's good to change. Good to feel
your blood pump. *(himself)* But where to? Where am I
going? *(old)* It don't matter. The road's what counts. Just
look at the road. Don't worry about where it's goin'.
(himself) I feel so trapped. So fucking unsure. Everything's
a mystery. I had it all in the palm of my hand. The gold, the
silver. I knew. I was sure. How could it slip away like that?
(old) It'll come back. *(himself)* But I'm not a true Marker no
more. Not really. They're all countin' on me. The bookies,
the agents, the Keepers. I'm a fucking industry. I even
affect the stocks and bonds. *(old)* You're just a man, Hoss.
Just a man. *(himself)* Yeah, maybe you're right. I'm just a
man.

(CHEYENNE *enters.)*

CHEYENNE: Hoss. He's here.

(HOSS *stays seated, relaxed. He has an air of complete acceptance.*)

HOSS: Good. He's here. That's good. What's his name?

CHEYENNE: He calls himself Crow.

HOSS: Crow. That's a good name. Did you sound him on the duel?

CHEYENNE: Yeah. He's game. He looks tougher than I thought, Hoss.

HOSS: Tough. Tough? *(he laughs)* Good. A tough Crow.

CHEYENNE: What'll I tell him?

HOSS: Tell him I like his style. Tell him I'm very tired right now and I'm gonna cop some z's. He can take a swim, have a sauna and a massage, some drinks, watch a movie, have a girl, dope, whatever he wants. Tell him to relax. I'll see him when I come to.

CHEYENNE: O.K. You all right, Hoss?

HOSS: Yeah. Just tired. Just a little tired.

CHEYENNE: O.K.

HOSS: Thanks, man.

CHEYENNE: Sure.

(CHEYENNE *exits.* HOSS *stays seated looking out.*)

HOSS: Maybe the night'll roll in. A New Mexico night. All gold and red and blue. That would be nice. A long slow New Mexico night. Put that in your dream, Hoss, and sleep tight. Tomorrow you live or die.

END OF ACT ONE

ACT TWO

SCENE: *The stage is the same. The lights come up on* CROW. *He looks just like Keith Richard. He wears highheeled green rock and roll boots, tight greasy blue jeans, a tight yellow t-shirt, a green velvet coat, a shark tooth earring, a silver swastika hanging from his neck and a black eye-patch covering the left eye. He holds a short piece of silver chain in his hand and twirls it constantly, tossing it from hand to hand. He chews a stick of gum with violent chomps. He exudes violent arrogance and cruises the stage with true contempt. Sometimes he stops to examine the guns on the floor, or check out the knives and the dummy. Finally he winds up sitting in* HOSS's *chair. A pause as he chews gum at the audience.* HOSS *enters dressed the same as in Act One.* CROW *doesn't move or behave any different than when he was alone. They just stare at each other for a while.*

HOSS: My sleuth tells me you're drivin' a '58 Impala with a Vet underneath.

CROW: Razor, Leathers. Very razor.

HOSS: Did you rest up?

CROW: Got the molar chomps. Eyes stitched. You can vision what's sittin'. Very razor to cop z's sussin' me to be on the far end of the spectrum.

HOSS: It wasn't strategy man. I was really tired. You steal a lotta' energy from a distance.

CROW: No shrewd from this end either. We both bow to bigger fields.

HOSS: You wanna drink or somethin'?

CROW *(he laughs with a cackle)*: Lush in sun time gotta smell of lettuce or turn of the century. Sure Leathers, squeeze on the grape vine one time.

HOSS: White or red?

CROW: Blood.

HOSS: Be right back.

CROW: No slaves in this crib?

HOSS: They're all in the pool watchin' a movie.

CROW: Very Greek.

HOSS: Yeah. Just relax, I'll be right back.

(HOSS *exits.* CROW *gets up and walks around thinking out loud.)*

CROW: Very razor. Polished. A gleam to the movements. Weighs out in the eighties from first to third. Keen on the left side even though he's born on the right. Maybe forced his hand to change. Butched some instincts down. Work them through his high range. Cut at the gait. Heel-toe action rhythms of New Orleans. Can't suss that particular. That's well covered. Meshing patterns. Easy mistake here. Suss the bounce.

(CROW *tries to copy* HOSS's *walk. He goes back and forth across the stage practising different styles until he gets the exact one. It's important that he gets inside the feeling of* HOSS's *walk and not just the outer form.)*

Too heavy on the toe. Maybe work the shoulders down. Here's a mode. Three-four cut time copped from Keith Moon. Early. Very early. Now. Where's that pattern. Gotta be in the 'Happy Jack' album. Right around there. Triplets. Six-eight. Here it comes. Battery. Double bass talk. Fresh Cream influence. Where's that? Which track. Yeah. The old Skip James tunes. Question there. Right there. *(sings it)* 'I'm so glad, I'm so glad, I'm glad, I'm glad, I'm glad.' Yeah. Ancient. Inborn. Has to be a surgery. Grind down.

(He hears HOSS *coming and darts back to the chair and sits as though he'd never moved.* HOSS *enters with a bottle of red wine and two glasses. He hands one to* CROW *and then he pours himself one and sets the bottle down.)*

HOSS: Ya know I had a feeling you were comin' this way. A sense. I was onto a Gypsy pattern early yesterday. Even conjured going that way myself.

CROW: Cold, Leathers. Very icy. Back seat nights. Tuck and roll pillow time. You got fur on the skin in this trunk.

HOSS: Yeah, yeah. I'm just gettin' bored I guess. I want out.

CROW: I pattern a conflict to that line. The animal says no. The blood won't go the route. Re-do me right or wrong?

HOSS: Right I guess. Can't you back the language up, man. I'm too old to follow the flash.

CROW: Choose an argot Leathers. Singles or LPs. 45, 78, 33 1/3.

HOSS: I musta' misfed my data somehow. I thought you were raw, unschooled. Ya' know? I mean, maybe the training's changed since my time. Look, I wanna just sound you for a while before we get down to the cut. O.K.? You don't know how lonely it's been. I can talk to Cheyenne but we mostly reminisce of old kills. Ya' know? I don't get new information. I'm starving for new food. Ya' know? That don't mean I won't be game to mark you when the time comes. I don't sleep standin' up. Ya' know what I mean? It's just that I wanna find out what's going on. None of us knows. I'm surrounded by boobs who're still playin' in the sixties. That's where I figured you were. Earlier. I figured you for Beach Boys in fact.

CROW: That sand stayed on the beach with me. You can suss me in detail Leathers. What's your key?

HOSS: This is really weird, me learnin' from you. I mean I can't believe myself admitting it. Ya' know? I thought I could teach you somethin'. I thought you were playin' to the inside. Choosin' me off just to get in the door. I mean I know you must be Mojo's trigger, right?

CROW: De-rail Leathers. You're smokin' the track.

HOSS: Eyes traced a Nevada route. It don't matter. If you ain't from the Rootforce you're on the Killin' floor Jack. Anyway you cut it you're a corpse. So let's lay that one on the rack for now. Let's just suspend and stretch it out.

CROW: We can breathe thin or thick. The air is your genius.

HOSS: Good. Now, first I wanna find out how the Gypsy Killers feature the stars. Like me. How do I come off. Are we playin' to a packed house like the Keepers all say?

CROW (*he cackles*): Image shots are blown, man. No fuse to match the hole. Only power forces weigh the points in our match.

HOSS: You mean we're just ignored? Nobody's payin' attention?

CROW: We catch debris beams from your set. We scope it to our action then send it back to garbage game.

HOSS: Listen chump, a lotta' cats take this game serious. There's a lotta' good Markers in this league.

CROW: You chose ears against tongue Leathers. Not me, I can switch to suit. You wanna patter on my screen for a while?

HOSS: Sorry. It's just hard to take. If it's true. I don't believe we could be that cut off. How did it happen? We're playing in a vacuum? All these years. All the kills and no one's watching?

CROW: Watching takes a side seat. Outside. The Game hammered the outside.

HOSS: And now you hammer us with fucking indifference! This is incredible. It's just like I thought. The Outside is the Inside now.

CROW (*he cackles*): Harrison, Beatle did that ancient. It cuts a thinner slice with us. Roles fall to birth blood. We're star marked and playing inter-galactic modes. Some travel past earthbound and score on Venus, Neptune, Mars.

HOSS: How do you get to fucking Neptune in a '58 Impala!

CROW: How did you get to earth in a Maserati?

HOSS: There! Why'd you slip just then? Why'd you suddenly talk like a person? You're into a wider scope than I thought. You're playin' my time Gypsy but it ain't gonna work. And get the fuck outa' my chair!!

(CROW *slides out of the chair and starts walking around, twirling his chain and chomping his gum.* HOSS *sits down. He sips his wine. Slowly through the dialogue* CROW *starts to get into* HOSS'S *walk until he's doing it perfect.*)

CROW: Your tappets are knockin' rock-man. I sense an internal smokin' at the seams.

HOSS: Yeah, so this is how you play the game. A style match. I'm beginning to suss the mode. Very deadly but no show. Time is still down to the mark, kid. How's your feel for shivs anyway?

CROW: Breakdown lane. Side a' the road days.

HOSS: Yeah, well that's the way it's gonna be. I ain't used a blade myself for over ten years. I reckon it's even longer for you. Maybe never.

(HOSS *begins to switch into a kind of Cowboy-Western image.*)

I reckon you ain't never even seen a knife. A pup like you. Up in Utah we'd use yer kind fer skunk bait and throw away the skunk.

CROW: Throwin' to snake-eyes now Leathers.

HOSS: So you gambled your measly grub stake for a showdown with the champ. Ain't that pathetic. I said that before and I'll say it again. Pathetic.

(CROW *is getting nervous. He feels he's losing the match. He tries to force himself into the walk. He chews more desperately and twirls the chain faster.*)

You young guns comin' up outa' prairie stock and readin' dime novels over breakfast. Drippin' hot chocolate down yer zipper. Pathetic.

CROW: Time warps don't shift the purpose, just the style. You're clickin' door handles now. There'll be more paint on your side than mine.

HOSS: We'd drag you through the street fer a nickel. Naw. Wouldn't even waste the horse. Just break yer legs and leave ya' fer dog meat.

CROW: That's about all you'll get outa' second. Better shift it now Leathers.

(HOSS *shifts to 1920s gangster style.*)

HOSS: You mugs expect to horn in on our district and not have to pay da' price? Da' bosses don't sell out dat cheap to small-time racketeers. You gotta tow da' line punk or you'll wind up just like Mugsy.

(CROW *begins to feel more confident now that he's got* HOSS *to switch.*)

CROW: Good undertow. A riptide invisible moon shot. Very nice slide Leathers.

(HOSS *goes back to his own style.*)

HOSS: Don't give me that. I had you hurtin'. You were down on one knee Crow Bait. I saw you shakin'.

CROW: Fuel injected. Sometimes the skin deceives. Shows a
power ripple. Misconstrued Leathers.
(CROW is into HOSS's walk now and does it perfect.)
HOSS: You were fish tailin' all over the track meathead! I had
you tagged!
CROW: Posi-traction rear end. No pit stops the whole route.
Maybe you got a warp in your mirror.
HOSS: There's no fuckin' warp. You were down!
CROW: Sounds like a bad condenser. Points and plugs.
HOSS: Suck ass! I had you clean! And stop walkin' like that!
That's not the way you walk! That's the way I walk!
(CROW stops still. They stare at each other for a second.
HOSS *rises slow.)*
All right. I can handle this action but we need a Ref. I ain't
playin' unless we score.
CROW: It's your turf.
HOSS: Yeah, and it's stayin' that way. I'm gonna beat you
Gypsy. I'm gonna whip you so bad you'll wish we *had* done
the shivs. And then I'm gonna send you back with a mark
on your forehead. Just a mark that won't never heal.
CROW: You're crossin' wires now Leathers. My send is to lay you
cold. I'll play flat out to the myth but the blood runs when
the time comes.
HOSS: We'll see. You're well padded Crow Bait but the layers'll
peel like a skinned buck. I'm goin' to get a Ref now. You
best use the time to work out. You ain't got your chops
down. You're gonna need some sharpening up. When I get
back it's head to head till one's dead.
*(HOSS exits. The band starts the music to CROW's song. He
sings.)*
'Crow's Song'
CROW: What he doesn't know — the four winds blow
Just the same for him as me
We're clutchin' at the straw and no one knows the law
That keeps us lost at sea

But I believe in my mask — The man I made up is me
And I believe in my dance — And my destiny

I coulda' gone the route — of beggin' for my life
Crawlin' on my hands and knees
But there ain't no Gods or saviors who'll give you flesh
    and blood
It's time to squeeze the trigger
But I believe in my mask — The man I made up is me
And I believe in my dance — And my destiny

The killer time — will leave us on the line
Before the cards are dealt
It's a blindman's bluff — without the stuff
To reason or to tell

But I believe in my mask — The man I made up is me
And I believe in my dance — And my destiny
(The song ends. HOSS *enters with the* REFEREE. *He's dressed
just like an N.B.A. ref with black pants, striped shirt,
sneakers, a whistle, baseball cap and a huge score-board
which he sets up down right. He draws a big 'H' on the top
left side of the board and a big 'C' on the other. He
separates the letters with a line down the middle. As he goes
about his business* HOSS *talks to* CROW.)

HOSS: I suppose you wouldn't know what's happened to my
    people? Becky. Cheyenne, Doc, Star-Man — they're all gone.
    So's my short.
CROW: Lotsa' force concentration in this spot Leathers. Could be
    they got bumped out to another sphere. They'll be back
    when the furnace cools.
HOSS: I don't fancy tap dancers Crow Bait. I like both feet on the
    ground. Nailed. Joe Frazier mode.
CROW: I vision you brought the rule, man.
HOSS: Yeah. He's gonna see that things stay clean. Points
    scored and lost on deviation from the neutral field state.
CROW: I'd say you already broke the mercury in round one.
HOSS: That don't count! We start when he's ready.
CROW: I can't cipher why you wanna play this course, Leathers.
    It's a long way from shivs.
HOSS: Just to prove I ain't outside.
CROW: To me or you?

(HOSS considers for a second but shakes it off.)

HOSS: I don't know how it is with you but for me it's like looking down a long pipe. All the time figurin' that to be the total picture. You take your eye away for a second and see you been gyped.

CROW: 'Gyped' — coming from 'Gypsy'.

(Through all this the REF puts himself through several yoga positions and regulated breathing exercises, cracks his knuckles, shakes his legs out like a track star and runs in place.)

HOSS: I'm gonna have fun skinnin' you.

CROW: If narrow in the eye ball is your handicap then runnin' a gestalt match figures suicidal. Look, Leathers, may be best to run the blades and forget it.

HOSS: No! You ain't no better than me.

CROW: You smell loser, Leathers. This ain't your stompin' turf.

HOSS: We'll see.

CROW: It took me five seconds to suss your gait. I ran it down to Skip James via Ginger Baker. How long's it gonna take you to cop mine?

HOSS: I ain't a Warlock I'm a Marker.

CROW: So stick to steel. Pistols. How 'bout the ancient chicken? Maserati against the Chevy. That's fair.

HOSS: I see you turnin' me in. I ain't stupid. I'm stickin' with this route Gypsy and that's what you want so can the horseshit. There's no Marker on the planet can out-kill me with no kinda' weapon or machine. You'd die with the flag still in the air. That's straight on. But too easy. I'm tired of easy marks. I'm drawin' to the flush. I'm gonna leave you paralyzed alive. Amputated from the neck down.

CROW: Just like you.

HOSS: We'll see.

(REF wipes himself off with a towel and tests his whistle.)

REF: All right. Let's get the show on the road. We all know the rules. When the bell rings, come out swingin'. When it rings again go to your corners. No bear hugs, rabbit punches, body pins or holdin' on. If a man goes down we give him five and that's it. After that you can kick the shit out of him. Ready? Let's have it!

*(An off-stage bell rings. The band starts slow, low-keyed
lead guitar and bass music, it should be a lurking evil sound
like the 'Sister Morphine' cut on 'Sticky Fingers'.* HOSS *and*
CROW *begin to move to the music, not really dancing but
feeling the power in their movements through the music.
They each pick up microphones. They begin their assaults
just talking the words in rhythmic patterns, sometimes
going with the music, sometimes counterpointing it. As the
round progresses the music builds with drums and piano
coming in, maybe a rhythm guitar too. Their voices build so
that sometimes they sing the words or shout. The words
remain as intelligible as possible like a sort of talking
opera.)*

Round 1

CROW: Pants down. The moon show. Ass out the window. Belt
lash. Whip lash. Side slash to the kid with a lisp. The dumb
kid. The loser. The runt. The mutt. The shame kid. Kid on
his belly. Belly to the blacktop. Slide on the rooftop. Slide
through the parkin' lot. Slide kid. Shame kid. Slide. Slide.

HOSS: Never catch me with beer in my hand. Never caught me
with my pecker out. Never get caught. Never once. Never,
never. Fast on the hoof. Fast on the roof. Fast through the still
night. Faster than the headlight. Fast to the move.

CROW: Catch ya' outa' breath by the railroad track.

HOSS: Never got caught!

CROW: Catch ya' with yer pants down. Whip ya' with a belt. Whup
ya' up one side and down to the other. Whup ya' all night
long. Whup ya' to the train time. Leave ya' bleedin' and cryin'.
Leave ya' cryin' for Ma. All through the night. All through the
night long. Shame on the kid. Little dumb kid with a lisp in
his mouth. Bleedin' up one side and down to the other.

HOSS: No! Moved to a hard town. Moved in the midnight.

CROW: Comin' in a wet dream. Pissin' on the pillow. Naked on a
pillow. Naked in a bedroom. Naked in a bathroom. Beatin'
meat to the face in a mirror. Beatin' it raw. Beatin' till the
blood come. Pissin' blood on the floor. Hidin' dirty pictures.
Hide 'em from his Ma. Hide 'em from Pa. Hide 'em from the
teacher.

HOSS: Never did happen! You got a high heel. Step to the lisp.

Counter you, never me. Back steppin' Crow Bait. History don't cut it. History's in the pocket.

CROW: The marks show clean through. Look to the guard. That's where it hides. Lurkin' like a wet hawk. Scuffle mark. Belt mark. Tune to the rumble. The first to run. The shame kid. The first on his heel. Shame on the shame kid. Never live it down. Never show his true face. Last in line. Never face a showdown. Never meet a face-off. Never make a clean break. Long line a' losers.

(All the other characters from Act One come on dressed in purple cheerleader outfits. Each has a pom-pom in one hand and a big card with the word 'Victory' printed on it. They do a silent routine, mouthing the word 'Victory' over and over and shaking their pom-poms. They move around the stage doing a shuffle step and stupid routines just like at the football games. CROW and HOSS keep up the battle concentrating on each other. The REF bobs in and out between them, watching their moves closely like a fight ref.)

HOSS: Missed the whole era. Never touched the back seat.

CROW: Coughin' in the corner. Dyin' from pneumonia. Can't play after dinner. Lonely in a bedroom. Dyin' for attention. Starts to hit the small time. Knockin' over pay phones. Rollin' over Beethoven. Rockin' pneumonia. Beboppin' to the Fat Man. Drivin' to the small talk. Gotta make his big mark. Take a crack at the teacher. Find him in the can can. There he's doin' time time. Losin' like a wino. Got losin' on his mind. Got losin' all the time.

HOSS: You can't do that!

(At some point the cheerleaders all come down stage in a line, turn their backs on the audience, take their pants down and bend over bare assed. When the bell rings marking the end of the round, they all turn around and show the reverse side of their cards which has the word 'Fight' in big letters. Then they all hobble off with their pants around their ankles giggling like school kids.)

CROW: In the slammer he's a useless. But he does his schoolin'. Tries to keep a blind face. Storin' up his hate cells. Thinks he's got it comin'. Bangin' out the street signs. Tryin' to do his time time. Turns into a candy-cock just to get a reprieve. Lost in the long sleeve. Couldn't get a back up. So he takes his lock up. Calls it bitter medicine. Makes a sour face. Gotta pay his dues back. Fakin' like a guru. Finally gets his big chance and sucks the warden's dinger. Gotta be a good boy. Put away the stinger. Put away the gun boy. I'll take away your time. Just gimme some head boy. Just get down on your knees. Gimme some blow boy. I'll give ya' back the key. I'll give ya' back the key boy! Just get down on my thing boy! Just get down! Get on down! Get on down! Get down! Get down! Get down! Come on!

(The bell rings. The music stops. The cheerleaders flash their cards and exit. REF goes to the scoreboard and without hesitation chalks up a big mark for CROW. CROW lies flat on his back and relaxes completely. He looks like he's dead. HOSS paces around nervous.)

HOSS: What the fuck! What the fuck was that!
(*to the* REF) You call that fair? You're chalkin' that round up to him! On what fucking grounds!

REF: Good clean body punches. Nice left jab. Straight from the shoulder. Had you rocked on your heels two or three times. No doubt about it.

HOSS: Are you kiddin' me! If flash and intensity is what you want I can give you plenty a' that. I thought we were shootin' honest pool. This kid's a fuckin' fish man. Nothin' but flash. No heart. Look at him. Wasted on his back and I'm still smokin'.

REF *(looking at his watch):* Better get some rest. You got thirty seconds left.

HOSS: I don't need rest. I'm ready to rock. It's him that's stroked out on the fuckin' floor, not me. Look at him. How can you give him the round when he's in that kinda' shape.

REF: Good clean attack.

HOSS: Clean! You call that clean? He was pickin' at a past that ain't even there. Fantasy marks. Like a dog scratchin' on ice. I can play that way if I was a liar. The reason I brought you into this match was to keep everything above the table. How can you give points to a liar.

REF: I don't. I give 'em to the winner.
   (The bell rings. CROW *jumps to his feet. The band strikes a note.* HOSS *steps in. He speaks to the band.)*
HOSS: All right look. Can the music. This ain't Broadway. Let's get this down to the skinny.
REF: What's going on! Play the round!
HOSS: What'sa matter, Crowbait? Afraid to do it naked? Drop the echo stick and square me off.
CROW: You should be past roots on this scale, Leathers. Very retrograde.
HOSS: Don't gimme that. I wanna strip this down to what's necessary.
CROW *(laughing)*: Necessity?
REF: This is against the code. Either play this round or it's no match.
CROW: We'll walk this dance so long as sounds can push round three. Certain muscles have gone green on me, Leathers. You can cipher.
   (The bell rings again. HOSS *and* CROW *put down their mikes slowly and deliberately as though they both had knives and agreed instead to wrestle.* REF *moves around them. The band remains quiet.)*
Round Two
HOSS *(talking like an ancient delta blues singer)*: Chicago. Yeah, well I hear about all that kinda 'lectric machine gun music. All that kinda 'lectric shuffle, you dig? I hear you boys hook up in the toilet and play to da mirror all tru the night.
CROW *(nervously)*: Yeah. Well, you know, twelve bars goes a long way.
HOSS *(growing physically older)*: It come down a long way. It come down by every damn black back street you can move sideways through. 'Fore that even it was snakin' thru rubber plants. It had Cheetahs movin' to its rhythm. You dig?
CROW: Yeah. Sure. It's a matter a' course.
   *(*CROW *moves to get away from him as* HOSS *becomes a menacing ancient spirit. Like a voodoo man.)*
HOSS: Yo' 'yeah' is tryin' to shake a lie, boy. The radio's lost the

jungle. You can't hear that space 'tween the radio and the jungle.

CROW: It's in my blood. I got genius.

HOSS: Fast fingers don't mean they hold magic. That's lost to you, dude. That's somethin' sunk on another continent and I don't mean Atlantis. You can dig where the true rhymes hold down. Yo' blood know that if nothin' else.

CROW: Blood. Well listen, I need some spray on my callouses now and then, but it's not about endurance.

HOSS: Ha! Yo lost dew claw. Extra weight. You ain't come inside the South. You ain't even opened the door. The brass band contain yo' world a million times over.

CROW: Electricity brought it home. Without juice you'd be long forgot.

HOSS: Who's doin' the rememberin'? The fields opened up red in Georgia, South Carolina. A moan lasted years back then. The grey and blue went down like a harvest and what was left?

CROW: That scale hung itself short.

HOSS: What was left was the clarinet, the bass drum, the trumpet. The fixin's for a salad. All hung gold and black in the pawnshop window. All them niggers with their hollers hangin' echoes from the fields. All the secret messages sent through a day a' blazin' work.

CROW: I can't do nothing about that. I'm in a different time.

HOSS: And what brought their heads up off the cement? Not no Abraham Lincoln. Not no Emancipation. Not no John Brown. It was the gold and black behind them windows. The music of somethin' inside that no boss man could touch.

CROW: I touch down here, Leathers. Bring it to now.

HOSS: You'd like a free ride on a black man's back.

CROW: I got no guilt to conjure! Fence me with the present.

HOSS: But you miss the origins, milk face. Little Brother Montegomery with the keyboard on his back. The turpentine circuit. Piano ringin' through the woods. Back then you get hung you couldn't play the blues. Back when the boogie wasn't named and every cat house had a professor. Hookers movin' to the ivory tinkle. Diplomats and sailors gettin' laid side by side to the blues. Gettin' laid so bad the U.S. Navy have to close down Storyville. That's how the move began. King Oliver got Chicago talkin' New Orleans. Ma Rainey, Blind Lemon Jefferson. They all come and got the gangsters hoppin'.

CROW: I'm a Rocker, not a hick!

HOSS: You could use a little cow flop on yer shoes, boy. Yo' music's in yo' head. You a blind minstrel with a phoney shuffle. You got a wound gapin' 'tween the chords and the pickin'. Chuck Berry can't even mend you up. You doin' a pantomime in the eye of a hurricane. Ain't even got the sense to signal for help. You lost the barrelhouse, you lost the honkey-tonk. You lost your feelings in a suburban country club the first time they ask you to play 'Risin' River Blues' for the debutante ball. You ripped your own self off and now all you got is yo' poison to call yo' gift. You a punk chump with a sequin nose and you'll need more'n a Les Paul Gibson to bring you home.

(REF blows his whistle.)

REF: Hold it, hold it, hold it!

(HOSS snaps back to himself.)

HOSS: What's wrong?

REF: I don't know. Somethin's funny. Somethin's outa whack here. We'll call this one a draw.

HOSS: A draw!

REF: I can't make heads or tails outa this.

HOSS: I had him cut over both eyes!

REF: We leave it. Let's get on with round 3.

HOSS: Look at him! He's unconscious standin' up.

REF: Play the round!

(The bell rings. CROW jumps into action, dancing like Muhammad Ali. HOSS moves flatfooted trying to avoid him. CROW is now on the offensive. The music starts again.)

Round 3.

CROW: So ya' wanna be a rocker. Study the moves. Jerry Lee Lewis. Buy some blue suede shoes. Move yer head like Rod Stewart. Put yer ass in a grind. Talkin' sock it to it, get the image in line. Get the image in line boy. The fantasy rhyme. It's all over the streets and you can't buy the time. You can't buy the bebop. You can't buy the slide. Got the fantasy blues and no place to hide.

HOSS: O.K. this time I stay solid. You ain't suckin' me into jive rhythms. I got my own. I got my patterns. Original. I'm my own man. Original. I stand solid. It's just a matter of time. I'll wear you to the bone.

CROW: Collectin' the South. Collectin' the blues. Flat busted in Chicago and payin' yer dues.

HOSS: Kick it out fish face! This time you bleed!

(REF blows his whistle. The music stops.)

REF *(to HOSS)*: No clinches. This ain't a wrestling match.

HOSS: I was countering.

REF: Just keep daylight between ya'. Let's go.

(The music starts again. HOSS goes back to the offense.)

HOSS *(to REF)*: I was countering, man!

CROW: Ain't got his chops yet but listens to Hendricks. Ears in the stereo lappin' it up. Likes snortin' his horses too chicken to fix. Still gets a hard on but can't get it up.

HOSS: Backward tactics! I call a foul!

(REF blows his whistle again.)

REF: No stalls. Keep it movin'. Keep it movin'.

HOSS: I call a foul. He can't shift in midstream.

REF: Let's go, let's go.

HOSS: He can't do that!

(REF blows his whistle again. The music comes up.)

CROW: Can't get it sideways walkin' the dog. Tries trainin' his voice to sound like a frog. Sound like a Dylan, sound like a Jagger, sound like an earthquake all over the Fender. Wearin' a shag now, looks like a fag now. Can't get it together with chicks in the mag. Can't get it together for all of his tryin'. Can't get it together for fear that he's dyin'. Fear that he's crackin' busted in two. Busted in three parts. Busted in four. Busted and dyin' and cryin' for more. Busted and bleedin' all over the floor. All bleedin' and wasted and tryin' to score.

(REF blows his whistle.)

HOSS: What the fuck's wrong now?

REF: I'm gonna have to call that a T.K.O.

HOSS: Are you fuckin' crazy?

REF: That's the way I see it. The match is over.

HOSS: I ain't even started to make my move yet!

REF: Sorry.

(HOSS lets loose a bloodcurdling animal scream and runs to one of the pistols on the floor, picks it up and fires, emptying the gun into the REF. REF falls dead. HOSS should be out of control then snap himself back. He just stands there paralyzed and shaking.)

CROW: Now the Keepers'll be knockin' down your hickory, Leathers.

HOSS: Fuck 'em. Let 'em come. I'm a Gypsy now. Just like you.

CROW: Just like me?

HOSS: Yeah. Outside the game.

CROW: And into a bigger one. You think you can cope?

HOSS: With the Gypsies? Why not. You could teach me. I could pick it up fast.

CROW: You wanna be like me now?

HOSS: Not exactly. Just help me into the style. I'll develop my own image. I'm an original man. A one and only. I just need some help.

CROW: But I beat you cold. I don't owe you nothin'.

HOSS: All right. Look. I'll set you up with a new short and some threads in exchange for some lessons.

CROW: No throw Leathers.

HOSS: I'll give ya' all my weapons and throw in some dope. How's that?

CROW: Can't hack it.

HOSS: All right, what do you want? Anything. It's all yours.

(CROW pauses)

CROW: O.K. This is what I want. All your turf from Phoenix to San Berdoo clear up to Napa Valley and back. The whole shot. That's what I want.

(HOSS pauses for a while, stunned. Then a smile of recognition comes over him.)

HOSS: Now I get it. I should cut you in half right now. I shoulda' slit yer throat soon's you came through the door. You must be outa' yer fuckin' cake man! All my turf?! You know how long it's taken me to collect that ground. You know how many kills it's taken! I'm a fuckin' champion man. Not an amateur. All my turf! That's all I got.

CROW: Yer throwin' away yer reputation, so why not give me yer turf.

You got nothin' to lose. It won't do you no good once the keepers suss this murder.

HOSS: I still got power. The turf is my power. Without that I'm nothin'. I can survive without the image, but a Marker without no turf is just out to lunch.

CROW: I thought you wanted to cop Gypsy style.

HOSS: I do but I need my turf!

CROW: The Gypsies float their ground, man. Nobody sets up colors.

HOSS: *You* want it bad enough. What's a' matter with you. You movin' outa' Gypsy ranks?

CROW: Razor Leathers.

HOSS: Wait a minute. You tricked me. You wanna trade places with me? You had this planned right from the start.

CROW: Very razor. An even trade. I give you my style and I take your turf.

HOSS: That's easy for you and hard for me.

CROW: You got no choice.

HOSS: I could just move out like I am and keep everything. I could make it like that.

CROW: Try it.

HOSS: You got it all worked out don't ya, fish face? You run me through a few tricks, take everything I got and send me out to die like a chump. Well I ain't fallin' for it.

CROW: Then what're you gonna do?

HOSS: I'll think a' somethin'. What if we teamed up? Yeah! That's it! You, me and Cheyenne. We start a Gypsy pack.

CROW: I'm a solo man. So are you. We'd do each other in. Who'd be the leader?

HOSS: We don't need a leader. Cheyenne could be the leader.

CROW: Not on my time. Rip that one up, Leathers.

HOSS: How did this happen? This ain't the way it's supposed to happen. Why do you wanna be like me anyway. Look at me. Everything was going so good. I had everything at my fingertips. Now I'm outa' control. I'm pulled and pushed around from one image to another. Nothin' takes a solid form. Nothin' sure and final. Where do I stand! Where the fuck do I stand!

CROW: Alone, Leathers.

HOSS: Yeah, well I guess I don't got your smarts. That's for sure. You played me just right. Sucked me right into it. There's nothin' to do but call ya'. All right. The turf's yours. The whole shot. Now show me how to be a man.

CROW: A man's too hard, Leathers. Too many doors to that room. A Gypsy's easy. Here, chew on some sap.

(He hands HOSS *a stick of gum.* HOSS *chews it in a defeated way.)*
Bite down. Chew beyond yourself. That's what ya' wanna shoot for. Beyond. Walk like ya' got knives on yer heels. Talk like a fire. The eyes are important. First you gotta learn yer eyes. Now look here. Look in my eyes. Straight out.

*(*HOSS *stands close to* CROW's *face and looks in his eyes.* CROW *stares back.)*
No! Yer lookin' in. Back at yourself. You gotta look out. Straight into me and out the back a' my head. Like my eyes were tunnels goin' straight through to daylight. That's better. More. Cut me in half. Get mean. There's too much pity, man. Too much empathy. That's not the target. Use yer eyes like a weapon. Not defensive. Offensive. Always on the offense. You gotta get this down. You can paralyze a mark with a good set of eyes.

HOSS: How's that?

CROW: Better. Get down to it. Too much searchin'. I got no answers. Go beyond confidence. Beyond loathing. Just kill with the eyes. That's it. That's better. Now. How do you feel?

HOSS: Paralyzed.

CROW: That'll change. The power'll shift to the other side. Feel it?

HOSS: No.

CROW: It'll come. Just hang in there. Feel it now?

HOSS: No. Can I blink now?

CROW: Yeah. Give 'em a rest.

*(*HOSS *blinks his eyes and moves away.)*
It'll come. You gotta practise like a musician. You don't learn all yer licks in one session. Now try out yer walk. Start movin' to a different drummer man. Ginger Baker's burned down. Get into Danny Richmond, Sonny Murray, Tony Williams. One a' them cats. More Jazz licks. Check out Mongo Santamaria, he might get yer heels burnin'.

*(*HOSS *starts moving awkwardly around the stage.)*

HOSS: I never heard a' them guys.

CROW: O.K. pick one. Any one. Pick one ya' like.

HOSS: Capaldi.

CROW: Too clean man. Try out Ainsley Dunbar. Nice hot licks. Anyone that gets the knife goin'. You gotta slice blacktop man. Melt asphalt.

HOSS: Keith Moon.

CROW: Too much flash. Get off the cymbals. Stop flyin' around the kit. Get down to it. Get down.

HOSS: Buddy Miles.

CROW: Just loud, man. Blind strength but no touch.

HOSS: Let's go on to somethin' else.

CROW: O.K. Body moves. Do a few chick moves. Fluff up yer feathers. Side a' the head shots. Hand on the hip. Let the weight slide to one side. Straight leg and the opposite bent. Pull on yer basket. *(HOSS tries to follow. CROW acts out all the gestures with a slick cool.)*
Spit out yer teeth. Ear pulls. Nose pulls. Pull out a booger. Slow scratches from shoulder to belly. Hitch up yer shirt. Sex man. Tighten your ass. Tighten one cheek and loosen the other. Play off yer thighs to yer calves. Get it all talkin' a language.

HOSS: Slow down! I ain't a fuckin' machine.

crow: Yer gettin' it. Yer doin' O.K. It's comin'. Talk to yer blood. Get it together. Get it runnin' hot on the left side and cold on the right. Now split it. Now put it in halves. Get the top half churnin', the bottom relaxed. Control, Leathers. Ya' gotta learn control. Pull it together.

HOSS: I'm not prepared. I can't just plunge into this. I gotta have some preliminaries.

CROW: O.K. You're right. Tell ya' what. Sit down in the chair and relax. Just take it easy. Come on.

HOSS: Maybe I'm too old.

CROW: Come on, just sit yerself down.
(HOSS sits in the chair. CROW paces around him.)
We gotta break yer patterns down, Leathers. Too many bad habits. Re-program the tapes. Now just relax. Start breathin' deep and slow. Empty your head. Shift your attention to immediate sounds. The floor. The space around you. The sound of your heart. Keep away from fantasy. Shake off the image. No pictures just pure focus. How does it feel?

HOSS: I don't know. Different I guess.

CROW: Just ease down. Let everything go.

(BECKY *comes on down left facing the audience. She wears a black wig and is dressed like Anna Karina in 'Alphaville'. She caresses herself as though her hands were a man's, feeling her tits, her thighs, her waist. Sometimes when one hand seems to take too much advantage she seizes it with the other hand and pushes it away.* HOSS *seems to turn into a little boy.)*

HOSS: You won't let nobody hurt me will ya'?

CROW: Nobody's gonna hurt ya'.

HOSS: Where have I been. All this time. No memory. I was never there.

(BECKY *talks straight out to the audience. But directs it at* HOSS.)

BECKY: I never knew you were that kind of a guy. I thought you were nice. A nice guy. I never thought you'd be like the others. Why do you do that? You know I'm not that kind of a girl. Come on. I just wanna talk. I wanna have a conversation. Tell me about yourself. Come on. Don't do that. Can't we just talk or something. All right, I wanna go then. Take me home. Come on. Let's go get a Coke. Come on. I mean it. Don't do that! Don't!

(Her hands pull off her sweater. The wig comes off with it. She's wearing a stiff white bra underneath. She struggles against her hands then lets them go then struggles again.)

Can't we go back? I'm going to be late. Can't we just kiss? No! Don't! Come on. I don't wanna do this. I'm not that kind of a girl. Look, just keep your hands off! I mean it. I don't like it. I just wanna talk. Tell me something nice.

(Her hands rip off her bra and feel her tits.)

Just talk to me. Tell me about your car. What kind of an engine has it got? Come on. Don't! Do you go racing a lot? Don't you take it down to the strip. No! Don't do that! Has it got overhead lifters. I really like those fat tires. They're really boss. Cut it out! No! Stop it! Don't!

(Her hands unzip her skirt and tear it off. One hand tries to get inside her panties while the other hand fights it off.)

I don't go all the way. I can't. I've never ever gone this far before. I don't wanna go all the way. I'm not that kind of a girl. I'll get pregnant. Stop it! All right, just get away from me! Get away! I'm getting out. Let me outa' the car! Let me out! Don't! Let go of me! Let go! *(she starts screaming)* Let me out! Let me out! Let me out! Let me out!

(She picks up her clothes and runs off.)

CROW: How is it now?

HOSS: I don't know. Trapped. Defeated. Shot down.

CROW: Just a wave. Time to scoop a Gypsy shot. Start with a clean screen. Are you blank now?

HOSS: I guess.

CROW: Good. Now vision him comin'. Walking towards you from a distance. Can't make out the face yet. Just feel his form. Get down his animal. Like a cat. Lethal and silent. Comin' from far off. Takin' his time. Pull him to ya'. Can you feel him?

HOSS: I think so. It's me. He's just like me only younger. More dangerous. Takes bigger chances. No doubt. No fear.

CROW: Keep him comin'. Pull him into ya'. Put on his gestures. Wear him like a suit a' clothes.

HOSS: Yeah. It *is* me. Just like I always wanted to be.

(The band starts playing the first two chords to 'Slips Away'.
CHEYENNE, STAR-MAN, DOC *and* GALACTIC JACK *come on dressed in white tuxedos with pink carnations in their lapels. They stand in a tight group and sing harmony notes to the music. They move in perfect choreographed movements like the old A capella bands. The music should build slowly with* HOSS's *voice until he stops talking and the* SINGERS *go right into the song.)*

Mean and tough and cool. Untouchable. A true killer. Don't take no shit from nobody. True to his heart. True to his voice. Everything's whole and unshakable. His eyes cut through the jive. He knows his own fate. Beyond doubt. True courage in every move. Trusts every action to be what it is. Knows where he stands. Lives by a code. His own code. Knows something timeless. Unending trust in himself. No hesitation. Beyond pride or modesty. Speaks the truth without trying. Can't do anything false. Lived out his fantasies. Plunged into fear and come out the other side. Died a million deaths.

Tortured and pampered. Holds no grudge. No blame. No guilt. Laughs with his whole being. Passed beyond tears. Beyond ache for the world. Pitiless. Indifferent and riding a state of grace. It ain't me! IT AIN'T ME! IT AIN'T ME! IT AIN'T ME!!

(He collapses in a ball and holds himself tight. The FOUR GUYS *sing.)*

'Slips Away'

FOUR GUYS: I saw my face in yours — I took you for myself
I took you by mistake — for me
I learned your walk and talk — I learned your mouth
I learned the secrets in your eye

But now I find the feelin' slips away
What's with me night and day is gone

Where you left off and I begin
It took me time to break the line
And on your own is tough enough
Without the thread that we got broken

But now I find the feelin' slips away
What's with me night and day is gone

If we could signify from far away
Just close enough to get the touch
You'd find your face in mine
And all my faces tryin' to bring you back to me

But now I find the feelin' slips away
What's with me night and day is gone
(repeat chorus)
(The song ends. The FOUR GUYS *exit.)*

CROW: Hey, Leathers. Come on man it's time to cope. Get ready to bop. The world's waitin'.

*(*HOSS *doesn't move.)*

Leathers, you gotta move out to it now. I taught ya' all I know. Now it's up to you. You got the power.

*(*HOSS *rises holding the gun in his hand.)*

HOSS: In the palm a' my hand. I got the last say.

CROW: That's it. Get ready to roll. You're gonna knock 'em dead.

HOSS: Knock 'em dead.

CROW: Yeah. What about it.

HOSS: You know somethin' Crow? I really like you. I really have respect for you. You know who you are and you don't give a shit.

CROW: Thanks, Leathers.

HOSS: I just hope you never see yourself from the outside. Just a flash of what you're really like. A pitiful flash.

CROW: Like you?

HOSS: Like me.

CROW: No chance, Leathers. The image is my survival kit.

HOSS: Survival. Yeah. You'll last a long time Crow. A real long time. You're a master adapter. A visionary adapter.

CROW: Switch to suit, Leathers, and mark to kill.

HOSS: Tough as a blind man.

CROW: Tough enough to beat the champ.

HOSS: Yeah. You win all right. All this. Body and soul. All this invisible gold. All this collection of torture. It's all yours. You're the winner and I'm the loser. That's the way it stands. But I'm losin' big, Crow Bait. I'm losin' to the big power. All the way. I couldn't take my life in my hands while I was alive but now I can take it in death. I'm a born Marker Crow Bait. That's more than you'll ever be. Now stand back and watch some true style. The mark of a lifetime. A true gesture that won't never cheat on itself 'cause it's the last of its kind. It can't be taught or copied or stolen or sold. It's mine. An original. It's my life and my death in one clean shot. *(HOSS turns his back to the audience. And puts the gun in his mouth. He raises one hand high in the air and pulls the trigger with the other. He falls in a heap. This gesture should not be in slow motion or use any jive theatrical gimmicks other than the actor's own courage on stage. To save the actor's face from powder burns an off-stage gun should be fired at the right moment.* CROW *stands silent for a while.)*

CROW: Perfect, Leathers. Perfect. A genius mark. I gotta hand it to ya'. It took ya' long enough but you slid right home. *(He calls off stage)* All right! Let's go!

*(*BECKY *and* CHEYENNE *enter, dressed like they were in Act One.)*

Becky, get some biceps to drag out these stiffs. Get the place lookin' a little decent. We're gonna have us a celebration.

BECKY: I had a feeling you'd take him. Was it hard?

CROW: Yeah. He was pretty tough. Went out in the old style. Clung right up to the drop.

BECKY: He was a good Marker man. One a' the great ones.

CROW: Not great enough.

BECKY: I guess not.

(She exits. CROW *talks to* CHEYENNE *who eyes him.)*

CROW: You eye me bitter wheel-boy. What's the skinny?

CHEYENNE: I guess you want me to drive for you now.

CROW: Maybe I hear you're the top handler in the gold circuit.

CHEYENNE: You hear good.

CROW: I cipher you turnin' sour though. Suicidal like the master. I don't fashion goin' down to a Kami-Kazi collision just after I knock the top.

CHEYENNE: You're cuttin' me loose?

CROW: That's it.

CHEYENNE: You got big shoes to fill Gypsy. They'll be comin' for you next.

CROW: Naw. That's fer lames. I'm throwin' the shoes away. I'm runnin' flat out to a new course.

CHEYENNE *(looking at* HOSS's *body)*: He was knockin' at the door. He was right up there. He came the long route. Not like you. He earned his style. He was a Marker. A true Marker.

CROW: He was backed up by his own suction, man. Didn't answer to no name but loser. All that power goin' backwards. It's good he shut the oven. If he hadn't he'd be blowin' poison in non-directions. I did him a favor. Now the power shifts and sits till a bigger wind blows. Not in my life run but one to come. And all the ones after that. Changin' hands like a snake dance to heaven. This is my time Cowboy and I'm runnin' it up the middle. You best grab your ticket and leave the Maserati with the keys.

CHEYENNE: Sure.

(He reaches in his pocket and pulls out the keys to the car.)
Good luck.
(He throws the keys at CROW'S *feet and exits.* CROW *smiles, bends down slowly and picks up the keys. He tosses them in his hand. The band starts the music.* CROW *sings 'Rollin' Down'.*
'Rollin' Down'
CROW: Keep me rollin' down
    Keep me rollin' down
    Keep me in my state a' grace
    Just keep me rollin' down

    I've fooled the Devil's hand
    I've fooled the Ace of Spades
    I've called the bluff in God's own face
    Now keep me from my fate

    If I'm a fool then keep me blind
    I'd rather feel my way
    If I'm a tool for a bigger game
    You better get down — you better get down and pray

    Just keep me rollin' down
    Keep me rollin' down
    Keep me in my state a' grace
    Just keep me rollin' down.
    (The song ends. The lights go to black.)

'The Way Things Are'

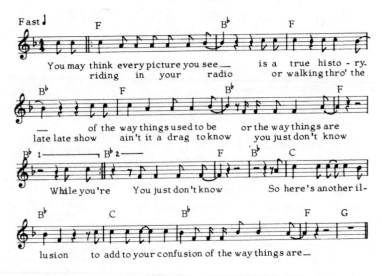

You may think every picture you see__ is a true histo - ry_
riding in your radio or walking thro' the

__ of the way things used to be or the way things are
late late show ain't it a drag to know you just don't know

While you're You just don't know So here's another il-

lu sion to add to your confusion of the way things are__

'Cold Killer'

'Becky's Song'

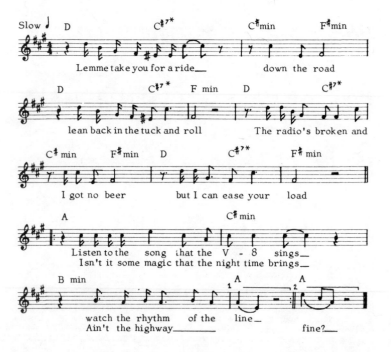

Lemme take you for a ride__ down the road
lean back in the tuck and roll The radio's broken and
I got no beer but I can ease your load
Listen to the song that the V - 8 sings__
Isn't it some magic that the night time brings__
watch the rhythm of the line__
Ain't the highway_____ fine?__

'Crow's Song'

What he doesn't know the four winds blow
We're clutching at the straw and noone knows the law

just the same for him as me But I believe in my
that keeps us lost at sea

mask The man I made up is me

And I believe in my dance And my destiny—

'Slips Away'

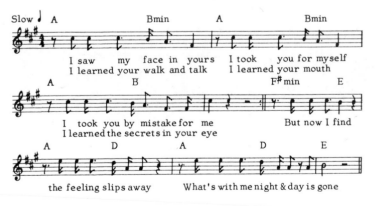

I saw my face in yours I took you for myself
I learned your walk and talk I learned your mouth

I took you by mistake for me But now I find
I learned the secrets in your eye

the feeling slips away What's with me night & day is gone

'Rollin' Down'

Geography of a Horse Dreamer

A Mystery in Two Acts

The play was first performed at the Theatre Upstairs on 21st February 1974 directed by the author.

ACT ONE: THE SLUMP

SCENE: *An old sleazy hotel room. Semi-realistic with a beat-up brass bed, cracked mirror, broken-down chairs, small desk etc. It's the dead of winter. A small paraffin heater provides the only heat.* CODY *lies spreadeagled on his back on the bed with his arms and legs handcuffed to each bed post. He's asleep with dark glasses on. He wears jeans and a cowboy shirt.* SANTEE *sits in a chair stage right of the bed reading the Racing Form. He wears a long dark overcoat, shiny black shoes and a gangster-type hat. In his lap is a Colt 45.* BEAUJO *is practising his pool shots with a cue and three balls on the floor. He wears a forties-type pinstriped suit with white shoes. His clothes are very wrinkled like he's been sleeping in them for a month. The stage should be dark or hidden before the opening. In the darkness the sound of horses galloping at a distance is heard. A slow-motion color film clip of a horse race is projected just above* CODY'S *head on the rear wall. No screen. The film begins out of focus and slowly is pulled into a sharp picture as the sound of galloping horses grows louder. The film clip lasts for a short while with the sound then* CODY *wakes up with a yell. The film goes off and the lights on stage bang up.* SANTEE *and* BEAUJO *continue their routines.*

CODY: Silky Sullivan in the seventh! By a neck. By a short head. Silky Sullivan in the seventh!

BEAUJO: He's got one, Santee.

SANTEE *(without moving from behind his paper)*: He's lost it. I told ya' he's lost it.

BEAUJO: Sounds very certain to me.

SANTEE: Silky Sullivan was a fly-by-night C.V. Whitney nag outa' Santa Anita. Won a couple a' stakes back in '62. Retired to stud shortly thereafter. Known chiefly for his dramatic closing rushes.

BEAUJO: I'll be darned. He's sure slippin' bad ain't he.

SANTEE: Slippin' ain't the word for it. He's almost disappeared.

CODY *(waking up)*: I need a better situation. It's too jagged in here. This wall-paper, the smell. You gotta take these things into consideration.

BEAUJO: Maybe he's right Santee.

SANTEE: Sure he's right. I'd be the first to agree that he's right. But it's his own damn fault. We was set up pretty in California weren't we. The Beverly Wilshire. Room service. The whole fandango.

BEAUJO: Yeah. Couldn't even hear yerself walk down the halls.

SANTEE: So what're we doin' here then?

BEAUJO: Fingers.

SANTEE: Naw, you numbskull. It ain't Fingers. That's a by-product of the situation. The reason we is here is on account of Mr. Artistic Cowboy here. Backslidin' on his system. That's the reason. If he was still dreamin' the winners we'd still be in California. In the money. Now ain't that right.

BEAUJO: I suppose so.

SANTEE: No supposin' about it. It's him that put us on the skids.

CODY: Could I have a cigarette?

SANTEE: We're runnin' low pal.

CODY: Just a puff then.

SANTEE: All right, give him a smoke.

BEAUJO: Could I have the keys.

(SANTEE reaches in his pocket and pulls out a ring of keys. He tosses them to BEAUJO)

SANTEE: Just the right arm.

(BEAUJO unlocks the handcuffs on CODY's right arm and gives him a cigarette then lights it. CODY smokes.)

SANTEE: You gotta remember that I ain't the source a' this caper Beaujo. I been askin' Fingers for a new dreamer for months now. It ain't my idea of a good time beatin' a dead horse ya' know.

BEAUJO: What's Fingers' angle keepin' Cody on then?

CODY: 'Cause I'm the best. He knows that. I'm the best.

SANTEE *(to* CODY*)*: Aw Shaddup! *(To* BEAUJO*)* You know a big time gamblin' man can't forget his early wins. All those memories when it was pourin' in like a flood. A quarter of a million bucks in a day. That ain't shootin' chicken ya' know.

BEAUJO: Yeah, but he must have other dreamers workin' for him. He's gotta pay the rent.

SANTEE: Sure he does but they're all mediocre. No class. I'll have to hand it to Mr. Artistic here, once upon a time he had some class.

CODY: I could regain my form if I got some decent treatment.

SANTEE: You had your shot at the red carpet routine and you blew it.

CODY: Nothin' fancy. Just some free movement during the day. A chance to get my blood moving again.

SANTEE: A chance to escape you mean.

CODY: I been with it too long Santee. I couldn't run out on ya' now. I'd be lost. It's been years. I been blindfolded and shuffled from one hotel to another for as long as I can remember. I ain't seen Great Nature for years now. The sun would probably blind me. Where would I go if I did escape?

SANTEE: Wherever you was headed last time you cut loose.

CODY: I don't remember that. I musta' been off my cake. I'd never try it again. I promise.

SANTEE: No dice Beethoven.

BEAUJO: Wouldn't hurt to just let him walk around the room here, Santee. Just to get his circulation going.

SANTEE: Well if it ain't the soft-hearted gangster type. Go ahead then! Turn him loose. I'm gettin' sick of his corny mug and his crucified position. Go ahead! Just remember if he gets loose it's your ass, not mine.

BEAUJO *(as he unlocks* CODY*)*: Sure, sure. The last time Fingers bothered with us was last Christmas when he gave us each an Indian-head nickel. We could be mistaken about this whole deal ya' know, Santee. I mean what if Fingers has just cut out on us. Left us here like a bunch a' saps.

SANTEE: He wouldn't do that.

BEAUJO: What's to stop him. He ain't exactly a man of high morals or nothin'.

SANTEE: Don't start bad-mouthin' Fingers now. Just 'cause things get tough is no reason to commit mutiny. Fingers's been good to us right along.

BEAUJO: Yeah, well I wouldn't exactly describe our present situation as the berries.

SANTEE: You got no faith. No gamblin' heart.

BEAUJO: I figure it's more like a game a' pool. You know, the way sometimes you got the feel. You got the touch. All the practice and technique in the world can't beat ya' cause you got magic. There's no trace a' tension. Then it goes. Just like that. No way to pin it down. It just slides away from ya'. I figure that's how it is with Cody here.

SANTEE: Maybe.

CODY: Yeah. That's how it is all right. The dreams are jagged. I get a fuzzy picture. Sometimes the numbers blur.

SANTEE *(to* CODY*)*: You'd agree with anything to get yerself off the hook. Come on, take a walk Mr. Artist. It may be yer last for a while.

*(*CODY *begins to get up from the bed. He struggles to gain muscular control, moving his limbs very slowly and trying to figure out how they work.* BEAUJO *backs away and lights a cigarette.* SANTEE *waves the pistol at* CODY*.)*

SANTEE: Just remember the old iron here. She gets very ticklish in a nervous situation.

BEAUJO: What if we was to make a real effort to treat him decent for a change. You know, steak and eggs in the morning, maybe a walk down the hallway, maybe even bring in a little Chippie to warm his heart.

SANTEE: None a' that stuff. First thing you know he'll be crying about his record again. That's what got him started in his present slump if you'll recall.

CODY: My record? You still got my record don't ya' Santee?

SANTEE: What'd I tell ya'? Yeah, yeah. I still got yer record.

CODY: Just don't bust it or nothin'. You wouldn't bust it wouldya'?

SANTEE: I'll bust yer damn neck if ya' don't start walkin' around this room pretty soon. Come on, start hoofin'.

CODY: I gotta take it slow. Everything's like mush. It feels like jello in my veins.

SANTEE: Yeah, yeah. The Champeen Complainer.

(CODY *finally gets to his feet and moves very slowly around the room trying to adjust to walking. Every once in a while he loses his balance and* BEAUJO *helps him stay upright.)*

BEAUJO: I know you got somethin' against art, Santee, but maybe he's right ya' know. I mean maybe his dreamin' does take on a kind of an art form, the way he does it. It might need some special stuff to get him back in top form.

SANTEE: Like what special stuff?

CODY: Like a decent bed for one thing.

BEAUJO: Yeah. I mean that's important. A thing like that. After all, the bed is where he does his work. This thing's like sleepin' on a week old griddle cake *(kicking the bed)*.

SANTEE: We can't afford it. It's not within the budget.

CODY: Some fresh air.

BEAUJO: Now you can't begrudge a man a little fresh air once in a while.

SANTEE: We might arrange some fresh air. Maybe. He's gotta be blindfolded though. He can't know where he is. That's the chief thing that Fingers impressed upon us. He can't for a second know where he is outside the room he's locked up in. Otherwise it spoils the dreaming. He can't know the time either.

CODY: We've come a long way from the Beverly Wilshire haven't we?

SANTEE: A long way down.

CODY: No, I mean we're on a whole different continent here aren't we? I can feel it.

SANTEE: How can you feel it Mr. Sensitive?

CODY: We took a ship.

SANTEE: Don't start guessing. There's no way you can find out.

CODY: You've blocked up all the windows again.

SANTEE: That ain't so unusual. That's standard procedure.

CODY: They speak English here though. They speak English don't they?

SANTEE: No guessing goddamnit! Or it's back in the sack and no dinner!

BEAUJO: Take it easy Cody. No need to get Santee worked up.

SANTEE: Just keep walkin' meatball.

CODY: It's all right. Fingers's theory was good for the beginning but now it sucks dogs.

SANTEE: How's that?

CODY: He don't understand the area I have to dream in.

BEAUJO: There's nothing we can do about that now.

CODY: Not this area. The inside one. The space inside where the dream comes. It's gotta be created. That's what Fingers don't understand. He thinks it's just like it was when I started.

SANTEE: So what's so different now.

CODY: He's blocked up my senses. Everything forces itself on the space I need. There's too much chaos now. He'll never get a winner out of me till the space comes back.

SANTEE: What a crock a' shit. I never heard so much gobbledygook in my whole life.

CODY: What do you dream about, Santee?

SANTEE: I don't dream. I'm one a' those rare dreamless sleepers. I got no worries, no troubles to work out. Everything's hunky-dorey.

CODY: I dream about the Great Plains.

SANTEE: Well that's yer whole damn trouble! That ain't what yer gettin' paid for. Yer paid to dream about racehorses. That's all.

BEAUJO: Yeah Cody. Shit man, you gotta get down to business. We're goin' down the tubes in this dump while you dream about the Great Plains.

CODY: It'll get worse.

SANTEE: What! It can't get worse! Put him back in the cuffs! Go on! Back in the sack! I ain't gonna tolerate that kinda' stuff!

BEAUJO: Now take it easy Santee.

SANTEE: Back in the sack! I ain't takin' no more crap from this hick! I can't stand the sight of him. Back in the sack!
(BEAUJO *leads* CODY *back to the bed and helps him back into the position he was in before. Then he puts the handcuffs*

back on him and locks them all. CODY *doesn't resist.)*

SANTEE *(pacing around the room with his gun)*: I'm goin' straight
to the top. No more fartin' around. Tomorrow morning I'm
gonna call Fingers and get the low-down. This whole
situation stinks. It's driving me crazy. It's useless keepin' this
creep here. He ain't gonna come up with a horse. He ain't
come up with a horse for over six months. One bum dream
after another. He's lucky if he even dreams a horse in this
century let alone a winner tomorrow. I can't stand it. I'm
goin' down there now and call him. Right now. You got some
change Beaujo? Gimme some change.

BEAUJO: All right, all right. Take it easy though Santee. You don't
want him comin' down on us too hard. You might catch him
in a bad mood.

(BEAUJO hands SANTEE some change for the phone.)

SANTEE: I don't care how I catch him. We just gotta get outa' this
slump somehow. I'm just goin' down the block to a phone
booth. Don't let this jerk loose for a second.

BEAUJO: You got the keys.

SANTEE *(remembering he's in a position of power)*: Yeah. Right. I
got the keys and don't you forget it. I got the keys.

(SANTEE exits. BEAUJO speaks to CODY.)

BEAUJO: What the hell are you tryin' to pull? You know better
than to get Santee pissed off like that. We're all in this
together ya' know.

CODY: Yeah. Sorry.

BEAUJO: I mean it's mostly up to you ya' know. I mean the
dreaming end of it. You're actually the big shot in the
situation. You can call all the shots. All you gotta do is dream
right.

CODY: It ain't so easy Beaujo. I'm dried up. I need a break.

BEAUJO: Yeah, I can see that and I'm doin' everything I can to
make that happen. But in the meantime you gotta play it
cool. When Santee's nerves are on edge you gotta go slow.

CODY: If I could just talk to Fingers myself maybe I could
convince him. I can't talk to Santee. He hates my guts. He
don't understand my position. It's very delicate work,
dreaming a winner. You can't just close your eyes and bingo!,

it's there in front of you. It takes certain special conditions. A certain internal environment.

BEAUJO: Well how did it happen before? It used to be a snap for you.

CODY: I don't know. It was accidental. It just sort of came to me outa' the blue. You know how that is. At first it's all instinct. Now it's work.

BEAUJO: Yeah, but you can't explain that kinda' stuff to mugs like Santee and Fingers. They don't buy it. All they understand is results. The process don't interest them.

(BEAUJO lights a cigarette and walks around.)

CODY: If I could just listen to my record again. That's all. Just a couple of tracks off my record.

BEAUJO: No show. It drives Santee crazy. Besides, like he says, that's part of what got you goin' downhill.

CODY: He's nuts. In the beginning I came up with six fifteen to one shots in a row. Six of 'em. And all of 'em came from the music. It's a source of inspiration, Beaujo.

BEAUJO: It's just impossible right now. We gotta go slow. Maybe later we can sneak the music back into it.

CODY: Then tell me where we are at least. What country is this?

BEAUJO: Can't do it Cody. It's strictly against the rules.

CODY: It's stupid! It's really stupid! I'm dreaming American horses and we're probably in Morocco somewhere. It don't make sense. I gotta know where we are so's I can adjust. I've lost track of everything. I need some landmarks.

BEAUJO: Fingers says the dreams are a gift from God. It don't matter what country you dream in.

CODY: Fuck Fingers! I'm the dreamer. I oughta' know.

BEAUJO: I could describe the general area to you maybe. The neighborhood around the hotel.

CODY: That'd help. Anything would help.

BEAUJO: It's a city. We're in a certain area of a city. The workers wear handkerchiefs around their heads. Their main concern is getting laid. They use rough language and swagger their manhood around.

CODY: That could be anywhere.

BEAUJO: It's a gambling town. Racing all year round. It's the poor people who lose. Dozens of big bookmakers for every block. A few sheisters work a system. All of 'em work with high stakes. The government has hooks directly into the bookmakers. There's protection on every level except for the bums. The police are paid off by high syndicates. For the rich it's a sport. For the poor it's a disease.

CODY: That doesn't help. It don't put me in touch with anything. I need firm ground to stand on.

BEAUJO: That's all I can give you.

CODY: What kind of cars do they drive?

BEAUJO: No more. I overstepped my bounds already.

CODY: What do the cops look like?

BEAUJO: That's it Cody. No more.

CODY: If I could just take a walk. You think you can talk Santee into letting me have a short walk?

BEAUJO: We'll see.

CODY: Oh man, I wish I was dead.

BEAUJO: It'll pass.

CODY: I got a feeling I'll never see daylight again.

BEAUJO: Now come on. Don't go gettin' morbid about it. This is just a slump we're in. Fingers'll pull us out of it.

CODY: Fingers is in the same boat as us. We're like his mirror. We never see him but we're always in touch. When he's winning we're in the Beverly Wilshire. When he's losing we're in a dump like this.

BEAUJO: He's got other dreamers. As soon as things pick up he'll move us.

CODY: Why is he keepin' me on! I wanna go back to Wyoming and raise sheep. That's all I wanna do. I got no more tips. I'm from the Great Plains not the city. He's poisoned my dreams with these cities.

BEAUJO: You want a sleeper?

CODY: Yeah. Gimme four of 'em. The blue ones.

BEAUJO: Oh no. Last time you had four you didn't come around for three days. We thought we lost ya'.

CODY: Gimme three then.

BEAUJO: Two's enough. Put you in a nice light sleep. Who knows, you might even dream a winner.

CODY: Just gimme the pills!

(BEAUJO *hands* CODY *two sleeping pills and a glass of water.* CODY *gobbles them down.)*

BEAUJO: You know your problem Cody? You don't accept the situation. There's no way out. Even if you could escape you're too weak to get very far. Even if you got very far we'd know where to find you. You gotta give into it boy.

CODY: Yeah. Maybe you're right.

BEAUJO: You gotta use some smarts. If you just relaxed into it and accepted it then everything would come to you. We might even let you have a little more freedom. No blindfolds. Walks in the park. All that stuff would come to you.

CODY: Yeah. I keep thinking this is temporary. How long's it been going on anyway?

BEAUJO: No time hints. Just forget about the other possibilities. This is all you got.

CODY: I can't remember how it started.

BEAUJO: You had a dream.

CODY: Yeah. I had that big dream.

BEAUJO: Then you got publicized.

CODY: Yeah. Life magazine. Then my folks started cashin' in. My brothers.

BEAUJO: Then half the state of Wyoming. You were the hottest thing in the West. Then we nabbed you.

CODY: I was kidnapped.

BEAUJO: Well, not exactly.

CODY: I was wined and dined. Where was that?

(*Through this* CODY *is getting drowsy until he finally falls asleep.)*

BEAUJO: Hollywood Park. Aqueduct. Yonkers.

CODY: What happened?

BEAUJO: We had to keep you secret. Too many scabbies cashin' in.

CODY: I used to wake up and not know where I was. As long as I can remember.

BEAUJO: It'll be all right now. It'll all come back to you. *(melodramatically)* You'll find that special area. A huge blue space. In the distance you'll see 'em approaching the quarter-mile pole. The thunder of hooves. Whips flying. The

clubhouse turn. You'll get a sense of it again. It'll all come
back just like it used to. You'll see. You got magic Cody.
You'll see.

(CODY *falls into a deep sleep.* BEAUJO *gets up and walks
around. He comes to a stop and looks around the room.)*

BEAUJO *(to himself)*: Huh, for a second there I thought I was lost.

(SANTEE *enters and shuts the door behind him. He goes to the
heater shivering from the cold and rubbing his arms.)*

BEAUJO: Did ya' talk to Fingers?

SANTEE: More or less.

BEAUJO: What do ya' mean? What'd he say?

SANTEE: He wasn't there. I had to talk to Zonka.

BEAUJO: Zonka? What's he know?

SANTEE: He gave me a message direct from Fingers.

BEAUJO: What's the scoop?

SANTEE: Dogs.

BEAUJO: Dogs?

SANTEE: Dogs. Greyhounds.

BEAUJO: Greyhounds?!

SANTEE: We been relegated to the dog tracks. It's the most
humiliatin' experience of my whole career. All on account a'
that meathead!

BEAUJO: There must be some mistake.

SANTEE: Ain't no mistake. It come from the top. He's gotta start
dreamin' dogs. That's all there is to it.

BEAUJO: But he don't know a greyhound from a crocodile. This
kid's strictly a horse man.

SANTEE: I know, I know. It ain't my idea.

BEAUJO: He can't suddenly change his whole style a' dreaming
like that. It might kill him.

SANTEE: Well he's gonna have to or our ass is grass! Wake him
up.

BEAUJO: I just gave him two sleepers.

SANTEE: Wake him up! Here, take the keys and unlock him.

(BEAUJO *take the keys and unlocks* CODY. CODY *stays asleep.)*

BEAUJO: Jesus Christ, Santee, we're gonna kill him with this kind
of treatment. I'm tellin' ya'.

SANTEE: I could care less. As far as I can tell it's him that got us into this mess and it's him that'll get us out. All my life I been proud a' my position. I've carried a certain sense of honor with me but I'll be damned if I'm gonna carry it to the goddamn dog track.

BEAUJO: He's out cold Santee.

SANTEE: Wake him up! I don't care how ya' do it. I want him on his feet. I'm gonna drill him with dogs 'till he hears 'em barkin' in his ears.

(BEAUJO slaps CODY's face and tries to bring him around.)

BEAUJO: It's no good Santee. He's out like a light.

SANTEE: Great! That's just great. Now we're sunk. We're really sunk.

(BEAUJO leaves CODY sleeping on the bed. His arms and legs are free.)

BEAUJO: It might mean we're being let off the hook Santee. Eased-in grade.

SANTEE: Can't you understand that this is serious business. What's a' matter with you. Zonka told me if there's no results within the week that Fingers is sendin' the Doctor over here.

BEAUJO: The Doctor?

SANTEE: Yeah. You know what that means.

BEAUJO: He can't do that.

SANTEE: Yeah, well that's what's gonna happen if Cowboy don't pop up with some winners and fast.

BEAUJO: The Doctor? Fingers must be crazy. He was goin' to the pay window every day for a month and now he can turn on us like this?

SANTEE: That's the way it falls Beaujo.

(CODY lets out a loud voice then goes right back into sleep.)

CODY: Native dancer in the eighth!

SANTEE: He's gettin' more and more pathetic. Native Dancer musta' died in the fifties.

BEAUJO: I got faith in him Santee.

SANTEE: Faith! What good is that gonna do us? We need results! Right now. There's only one thing we can do.

(SANTEE goes to the racing form and leafs through it.)

We gotta take the gamble. We gotta try to pick some dogs ourselves and pass 'em off as his dreams. That's the only thing.

BEAUJO: But we don't even know how to read the form for greyhounds. You don't know the first thing about it.

SANTEE: We can learn. Look, it says here: 'Black Banjo, the young Walthamstow hopeful has been unlucky in his last six outings. With the advantage of trap one and a slow starter to his right, Black Banjo could get to the first bend and go clear.'

CODY: Man o' War by a neck!

SANTEE: Can you do something about him?

BEAUJO: He'll come around in a while.

SANTEE: Look, write these down. Get a piece a' paper and write.

BEAUJO: I don't know Santee. We're takin' quite a risk.

(BEAUJO goes to a small desk and gets a pad and pencil. He writes down what SANTEE says.)

SANTEE: It's worth a try. We might even pick us some winners. Put down: 'Harringay, 7.45, Sgt. Mick. 8.00, Go Astray. 8.15, Zeitung. 8.30, Lemon Castle. 8.45, Come Dark Night. 9.00 —

CODY *(speaking in an even, cool voice)*: Black Banjo will win the seventh race at Wimbledon by two and a half lengths on the trot.

SANTEE: Can you shut him up. I can't concentrate.

BEAUJO: Wait a minute! Did you hear what he said. Black Banjo! That's a dog. A greyhound!

SANTEE: I know. I just read it in the paper.

BEAUJO: He just picked him to win at Wimbledon.

SANTEE: So what. The power of suggestion. He musta' heard me read it.

CODY: Black Banjo, a young son of the great Irish stud dog Monalee Champion has all the looks and speed of a top-class dog. His early speed and clever tracking has told the tale on more than one occasion. Although unlucky in most of his recent deciders he will definitely win by two and a half lengths tonight at Wimbledon.

BEAUJO: Listen to that! Where'd he get information like that? Look it up. See if that's his breeding?

SANTEE: What'd he say?

BEAUJO: Monalee Champion. Look it up.

SANTEE *(looking in the paper)*: Monalee Champion. Let's see. Yeah. What do ya' know. Monalee Champion. How'd he know that?

BEAUJO: He's back on, Santee! He's back on the winners! We're gonna be in the money again!

SANTEE: You think so? I'd hate to risk it.

BEAUJO: I know it. I can feel it. He's havin' a breakthrough.

CODY: Black Banjo will break in front with Shara Dee close up at the first bend. There'll be some bad crowding going around and Stow Welcome will be thrown to the outside. From there to the wire Black Banjo will have it all his own way. Shara Dee will be closing in the final stages but will not come to terms with the winner. She will be second with another length back to Seaman's Pride.

SANTEE: Go call Fingers. If Zonka answers pass on the message. Black Banjo to win, Shara Dee to place. Forecast, one and three. Tell him it's a certainty.

BEAUJO: Right.

SANTEE: And grab me a fifth of Scotch on the way back. I'm gonna need it if we lose.

BEAUJO: This is it Santee. I feel it in my bones. The slump is over. Tomorrow we'll be sittin' pretty!

SANTEE: It ain't happened yet.

(BEAUJO exits. SANTEE talks quietly to CODY who remains asleep.)

O.K. Mr. Artistic. Maybe I was wrong. Maybe I was pushin' it too hard. This better be it boy or we're all gonna be cut up in little pieces and mailed to our Mommas. I know you ain't used to workin' under pressure but that's how it is. It's like a snake bitin' its own tail. We keep infecting each other. The Doctor's on our back. The pressure's there. It comes from the outside. Somewhere out there. We wind up with the effects. I don't understand how you work Beethoven, that's how come I got no patience. To me it's a lot a' mumbo-jumbo. Like I said, I don't even have no dreams. All I know is that you was right once. For a solid month you was right. You was so right that you had somebody out there eatin' turtle soup and fillet mignon three times a day. Being chauffer-driven to the grocery store. That's how it is. You got the genius, somebody else got the power. That's how it always is Beethoven. The most we can hope for is a little room service and a color T.V. *(CODY sits up. He talks with another voice; slightly Irish, as though he's been inhabited by a spirit.)*

CODY: The main mistake is watching the race in an emotional way. As though the dog you've gambled on is a piece of yourself. That way you only see one-sixth of the race and miss the other five dogs. You might go a dozen races gambling on dogs you've seen before but never watched.

SANTEE: Say, what is this? Are you awake now or what?

(CODY gets up off the bed and moves easily around the room.)

CODY: You gotta take mental photographs of each dog. You gotta draw back from the race, take an indifferent attitude. Memorize forty-eight dogs a night. Don't gamble for a week of racing. Just take photographs.

SANTEE: Don't try nothin' funny! I still got the rod.

CODY: Once you've built up an interior form you attack in a calculated way. Never let the odds influence you. Go about it cold-blooded. Make definite decisions and stick to them. Forget the Quinellas and Duellas. They're for suckers. Stick with £5 reverse forecasts, tenners each way on the selection.

SANTEE: What's got into you. Get back over here on the bed!

CODY: Keep a record of the seasonal dates of bitches. One week before they're due in season back 'em to the hilt. Don't be fooled by fast-improving pups but don't be afraid to have a gamble in the middle of their form. Forget Yellow Printer sons in the Derby. They're jinxed. Too difficult to tune them up. Look at Super Rory. Donemark Printer. Tremendous class but see how fast they blew out.

SANTEE: Shaddup!

(CODY snaps out of it back into his old self. He's barely able to stand up. A short silence then BEAUJO bursts in the door.)

BEAUJO: Fingers is comin!

SANTEE: What! Now?

CODY: Lemme talk to him.

BEAUJO: After the race. He's comin' right after the race.

SANTEE *(threatening* CODY*)*: You better be right Schmoe.

CODY: I gotta talk to him.

BEAUJO: He's bringin' the Doctor if he loses.

SANTEE: Where's my Scotch?

*(*CODY *collapses on the floor.* BEAUJO *hands* SANTEE *a fifth of Scotch.* SANTEE *breaks it open and takes a long swig. They both stare at* CODY *on the floor as the lights dim and the sound of an* ANNOUNCER'S VOICE *is heard over the speakers.)*

ANNOUNCER'S VOICE: The hare is running at Wimbledon. Black Banjo breaks clear of Shara Dee in trap three followed closely by Stow Welcome and Seaman's Pride. As they go into the first turn it's Black Banjo by a length and a half. There's some bad crowding. Stow Welcome is knocked out of it. Down the back straight it's Black Banjo going four lengths clear from Shara Dee, followed by Seaman's Pride. It's Black Banjo into the third bend still well clear of Shara Dee who is making up ground on the outside. Coming for home it's Black Banjo with Shara Dee closing very fast. It's Shara Dee and Black Banjo!

(The swelling sound of a huge crowd drowns out the ANNOUNCER'S VOICE *as the lights go to black.)*

END OF ACT ONE

ACT TWO: THE HUMP

SCENE: *A fancy hotel room with the furniture in the same position as in Act One. A color T.V. with a flickering image, the sound off. A record player on top of a chest of drawers. The characters all have new clothes but all in the same styles as Act One.* CODY *still wears his shades and speaks with a slight Irish accent. He stands center stage holding a fishing pole at arm's length with a white rabbit skin tied to the end of the line so it just touches the floor. He turns slowly in a tight circle so that the rabbit skin drags across the floor around him. He watches a litter of imaginary greyhound pups chasing the skin. This is the method for schooling puppies to chase the mechanical hare in a circle.* SANTEE *sits on a chair in the same position as Act One, reading the Racing Form.* BEAUJO *sits at a table down left dealing a hand of five card stud to himself and an imaginary partner across from him. In the darkness, before the action begins, the sound of dogs yapping is heard faintly and grows louder as a color film clip of greyhounds racing in slow motion is projected on the rear wall. It's done in the same way as the film of the horses at the beginning of Act One.* CODY *yells at his imaginary puppies, the film goes off and the lights on stage bang up.* CODY *turns in a circle and talks.* SANTEE *and* BEAUJO *ignore him.*

CODY: You gotta watch that brindle. He's a devil. The biggest in the litter. Thinks he can get away with murder. It's very crucial to catch them at an early age. Once they get the taste for fightin' there's the seed of a bad habit. It's usually the big ones that get pushy. You don't want to take the fire out of 'em. Just let 'em know that you'll have none of it.

(He strikes out at one of the puppies then goes on in a circle.)

SANTEE: I notice he missed the fifth at Catford yesterday.

BEAUJO: Seven out of eight ain't so bad.

SANTEE: Just hope it's not a bad omen.

BEAUJO: We're in the pink Santee. He's locked into it this time.

SANTEE: Yeah. It gives me the creeps. Like being a nurse at a flip house.

(CODY reverses direction with the pole and keeps moving in a tight circle.)

CODY: It's important to reverse your direction once in a while. To balance out the muscles. Too much counter-clockwise action makes 'em soft on the right side. You watch the Irish dogs. You'll never see near as many dogs breaking down in Ireland as you do in England. The schooling's different. We take more time in Ireland. More patience.

SANTEE: He still don't know where he is.

BEAUJO: He's gettin' closer though.

SANTEE: If ya' ask me he's further away than ever. He's off his cake Beaujo.

BEAUJO: Lucky for us.

SANTEE: What do ya' suppose happened to him?

BEAUJO: You got me. Some kinda' weird mental disorder. I told ya' he was a genius. There's a very fine line between madness and genius ya' know.

SANTEE: Yeah, yeah. Cut the baloney. He's gone bananas and that's all there is to it. It just happens to coincide with our needs.

BEAUJO: Well, leastwise Fingers is happy. That's all that counts right now.

(A loud knock at the door. SANTEE and BEAUJO leap to their feet. CODY keeps turning in a circle and mumbling to the puppies. SANTEE has his gun out.)

SANTEE: You expectin' company?

BEAUJO: Not me. Must be room service.

SANTEE: I didn't order nothin'.

BEAUJO: Me neither.

(More loud knocking.)

SANTEE: Well answer it! Go on!

(BEAUJO goes to the door.)

BEAUJO: Who is it?

DOCTOR'S VOICE: Fingers! Open up!

BEAUJO *(to* SANTEE*)*: Oh shit, it's Fingers!

SANTEE: Well let him in.

BEAUJO *(to the door)*: Hold on a second!

*(*BEAUJO *unlocks three or four locks on the door as* SANTEE *grabs the fishing pole out of* CODY'S *hand and hides it under the bed. He grabs* CODY *by the back of the neck and throws him on to the bed.* BEAUJO *swings the door open and* FINGERS *sweeps into the room with the* DOCTOR *behind him.* FINGERS *is tall, thin and rather effete wearing a bowler hat, tweed cape with matching trousers, black vest with a white carnation, thin pencil-line mustache, spats, black cane and gaudy rings on every finger including the thumbs. The* DOCTOR *is very fat and looks like Sydney Greenstreet. He wears all black in the style of the thirties and carries a doctor's ominous-looking black bag.)*

FINGERS: Good God man, you'd think it was Fort Knox in here the way you carry on with the bloody locks. Where's my boy?

BEAUJO: Sorry Fingers. We was takin' precautionary measures.

*(*FINGERS *spots* CODY *on the bed and moves towards him.* CODY *runs frantically to the other side of the room. He seems terrified of* FINGER'S *every move.)*

FINGERS: Ah yes! Yes, yes, yes! I should have known he'd have the look of eagles. Absolutely. Look at him Doctor. Just look. Splendid.

DOCTOR: Hmm. So that's him.

SANTEE: We been keepin' him good, Fingers. Three squares a day. Free movement through the room. Just like you said.

FINGERS: Those eyes. It almost hurts to look in his face.

SANTEE: You ain't kiddin'. I was just tellin' Beaujo how sick I was gettin' a' his mug.

(The DOCTOR *takes his coat off and throws it on the bed, then he helps* FINGERS *off with his cape.)*

FINGERS *(to* CODY*)*: At last we meet. Like the tail and the head of a great dragon. This calls for a celebration. Order some sherry and cognac. The finest in the house. *(To* CODY*)* You do drink I trust?

SANTEE: He ain't being too communicative lately Fingers. He's slipped into some kinda' depression or something.

(BEAUJO *rings for the* WAITER. *The* DOCTOR *sinks into a chair and watches T.V. He turns the sound up very loud.* FINGERS *glares at him.*)

FINGERS: Doctor! I say, Doctor!

(FINGERS *crosses briskly to the T.V. and turns the sound off. The* DOCTOR *just stares into the screen.*)

FINGERS: Do you mind? We're trying to conduct a conversation.

(FINGERS *crosses back to* SANTEE.)

Now then. Where are we? Oh yes. Depression. Depression? Good Lord, we can't have that. Let me feel his temperature.

(FINGERS *moves toward* CODY. CODY *leaps over the bed and crashes into a wall trying to get away from him. The* DOCTOR *is unmoved.*)

FINGERS: Is he always this hypertensive?

BEAUJO: Only around strangers. He's only seen me and Santee for the past year and a half now. He don't know what to make of you.

SANTEE: Yeah, he should settle down in a little while. Then you can pet him.

FINGERS: I see. Poor chap. I dare say he does look a bit at odds with himself doesn't he. Has he been sleeping well?

SANTEE: In spurts. He'll fall dead asleep for fifteen minutes in the middle of the floor and then wham, he'll be up and prowling the room again.

FINGERS: I don't like the sound of that at all. Doctor, did you hear that?

DOCTOR: I wasn't listening.

FINGERS: Santee says the poor fellow only sleeps for fifteen minutes at a stretch and then he's up and about.

DOCTOR: So what? It's not unusual in cases like this. People in his state can go a week without sleeping a wink.

FINGERS: I see. I rather thought it was more serious than that.

DOCTOR: 'Course they don't live long.

FINGERS: Then it is serious.

DOCTOR: Maybe, maybe not. Depends on the particular case.

FINGERS: Well I do wish you'd examine the poor chap and make some sort of diagnosis. After all our livelihood hinges upon his wellbeing.

DOCTOR: Later. Right now I'm gonna take in a little viewing.

FINGERS: Well I suppose it can wait. Now then, where's the champagne?

(SANTEE and BEAUJO seem surprised by FINGER'S lack of authority over the DOCTOR.)

BEAUJO: I thought you said sherry.

FINGERS: Did I? Ah yes, sherry. So I did.

CODY: Just two tablespoons full. That's all. Otherwise you blow 'em out.

FINGERS: Is he speaking to me?

SANTEE: We're never certain Fingers. It could be any of us.

FINGERS: I see. How long has this been going on.

BEAUJO: Even since the switch-over.

FINGERS: Switch-over?

SANTEE: To greyhounds.

BEAUJO: You upset something very fragile Fingers. He may never come back from it.

FINGERS: I'm afraid I don't understand.

BEAUJO: He's a horse dreamer Mr. Fingers. A horse dreamer. When you had us switch over to dogs something snapped in him. The mind is a very mysterious thing ya' know.

FINGERS: Yes, I see. I had no idea. Poor devil.

SANTEE: He's doin' all right though. He's still on the winners and everything.

BEAUJO: But it won't last for long.

SANTEE: Will you shut up!

BEAUJO: I'm only trying to give ya' fair warning so it don't come as too much of a shock.

SANTEE: Beaujo's talkin' through his hat Fingers. He don't know nothin' for certain.

FINGERS: It's all my fault. I should have brought a stop to this insanity long ago. I should have known something like this would happen.

SANTEE: Nothing's happened. We've been in the money for three weeks straight now. Everything's hunky-dorey Fingers. All we gotta do is ride him out. When he hits another slump we just give him a breather. Simple as that.

(A knock at the door.)

That must be the waiter. You just set yourself down on the bed there and I'll order us some drinks. You just relax Fingers. Everything's gonna be O.K. Beaujo, help him on to the bed. Take his shoes off, loosen his tie.

(BEAUJO *helps* FINGERS *to the bed.* FINGERS *has gone all weak and sickly now. Every time* FINGERS *moves,* CODY *moves frantically to get away from him, crashing over furniture and smashing into the walls. The* DOCTOR *remains indifferent, staring into the T.V. with the sound off.* SANTEE *opens the door and lets the* WAITER *in. The* WAITER *wears white gloves and tails. He looks a bit apprehensive about the situation.)*

WAITER: Uh, you rang sir?

SANTEE: Yeah, get us a coupla' bottles of yer best cognac and some sherry. Nothin' but the best. Oh yeah, and some glasses. Here's a tenner. Keep the change.

WAITER: Very good sir. Thank you very much sir.

SANTEE: Don't mention it. Now scram.

(He shoves the WAITER *out the door and bolts it.* FINGERS *is lying on the bed as* BEAUJO *takes* FINGER'S *shoes off and massages his feet.)*

FINGERS: I had a feeling it would end like this. I've committed a terrible sin.

SANTEE: Nothing's ended. It's all going on right now. We're on top. Nothing's ended Fingers.

CODY: The sickness is sweeping through the kennel! There's no escape! Intestinal Catarrh is on the march! Sprinters and stayers! Everyone's equal in this.

FINGERS: What in God's name is he on about?

SANTEE: It's nothin' Fingers. He's practisin' up for White City tonight.

FINGERS: Oh my God!

SANTEE: I'll have him under control in just a minute. Come here you!

(SANTEE *moves toward* CODY. CODY *leaps away again crashing into things like a frightened animal.)*

FINGERS: Don't you touch him! Don't you lay a hand on him! Enough damage has been done already.

CODY (*panting like a dog*): Didn't you give me enough stick already! At Dundalk! Shelbourne Park! Trucked around half of Ireland like so much hamburger.

FINGERS *(to* SANTEE*)*: Now you've done it! You've pushed him too far. He's over the edge.

CODY *(to* SANTEE *)*: I kept crying for trap one. Over and over again I asked for trap one. I could've won from the inside! But no, I was forced to go wide. You couldn't understand why I'd check at the third bend. Time and again I'd check at the third bend. How stupid can you get. I was schooled on the inside hare and you put me in trap six. Trap six! Trap six! Trap six! I'm bloody tired of trap six!

SANTEE: Aw fuck off ya' nut-case! *(to* FINGERS*)* I wash my hand a' this whole deal. I warned ya' right from the start about this country bumpkin. He's a weirdo. Unreliable. I coulda' found ya' plenty a' good dreamers from the city but no, we had to go to the middle of the goddamn Great Plains and bring back a dodo. A fruitcake. Well I've had it. From here on it's your ballgame. I'm watchin' T.V. with the Doc.

*(*SANTEE *goes and stands behind the* DOCTOR *and watches T.V.)*

BEAUJO *(to* FINGERS*)*: Maybe after White City tonight we should give him a rest Fingers. Let him get his strength back.

FINGERS *(sitting up on the edge of the bed)*: There'll be no White City tonight or any other night. I'm setting him free.

SANTEE: You're what! You can't do that! He's still worth millions even though he is crazy.

FINGERS *(getting up and moving toward the* DOCTOR*)*: I don't care what he's worth. He's going back tonight. Doctor, would you be so kind as to arrange air passage for two to Wyoming. I'm taking him back personally.

(The DOCTOR *stays staring at the T.V.* FINGERS *moves back to* BEAUJO. SANTEE *follows him.)*

SANTEE: Fingers, wait a minute. I take back what I said before.

FINGERS: We must gather his personal effects together.

BEAUJO: All he's got is what he's wearing and an old beat-up record.

FINGERS: Very well. Get it.

(BEAUJO *goes to a drawer and pulls out an old album with no cover.)*

SANTEE: This is a real mistake Fingers. Why don't we just keep him on until he starts slippin' again. No harm in that. He's a gold mine right now.

FINGERS: Gold mine. Yes. By the way, what was the name of that town we took him from. Do you remember?

BEAUJO: Somewhere in the High Mountain country. Above the Big Horns.

FINGERS: That's quite a large piece of real estate as I recall. Can't you be more specific.

BEAUJO: Something like Pawnee or Cheyenne. Something like that.

SANTEE: Cheyenne's in the south-east. It was north of there.

BEAUJO: Something like Arapohoe or Mitchell. Was it Mitchell?

FINGERS: Does anyone have a map?

SANTEE: Look, Fingers, just leave him to us for a while. Give him another chance. We'll bring him around.

BEAUJO: Well look, we can figure it out easy enough. We left Salt Lake City on a Friday night and drove all night. We crossed the Utah state line about two in the morning.

FINGERS: Yes, I remember that. I remember thinking, now we're in Wyoming, it can't be far now. On the map it looked to be no further than Brighton is from London. Then all the next day we drove and drove. I'd never seen such country. Nothing as far as the eye could see. Nothing.

BEAUJO: We hit the Wind River Reservation about noon. We had lunch in the Silver Star. Fingers bought a cowboy hat and a pair of spurs.

FINGERS: Yes! I remember that! I remember thinking this is the West! This is really The West! Then we got to that town where Buffalo Bill lived. I forgot the name of it. Oh what a town! Saloons with Winchester rifles tacked up on the walls. Real cowboys in leather chaps. Indians shuffling through the dusty streets. Buffalo Bill's name plastered on everything. And at night. At night it was magical. Like praying. I'd never heard such a silence as that. Nowhere on the earth. So vast and lonely. Just the brisk cold night blowing in through the hotel window. And outside, the blue peaks of the Big Horn mountains. The moon shining on their snowy caps. The prairie stretching out and out like a great ocean. I felt that God was with me then. The earth held me in its arms.

(A short pause as FINGERS *reflects.)*

BEAUJO: That was the town.

FINGERS: What was.

BEAUJO: The town we nabbed him in. That was it.

FINGERS: Yes! That's right! What was it called? Doctor, do you remember the name of that charming town. The one where Buffalo Bill lived. Doctor?

*(*FINGERS *turns to the* DOCTOR *who is sitting very still in a kind of trance.)*

For heaven's sake man, snap out of it.

SANTEE: What's eatin' him now.

*(*FINGERS *goes to the* DOCTOR *and shakes his shoulder.)*

FINGERS: I say. Doctor! I asked you to go and arrange our passage to Wyoming. Doctor!

*(*FINGERS *shakes him again. The* DOCTOR *lets out a bloodcurdling yell and throws* FINGERS *across the room.* CODY *screams like a dog who's being whipped. He whimpers in a corner.* BEAUJO *and* SANTEE *stand facing the* DOCTOR *who stands center stage.* FINGERS *moans on the floor holding his leg in pain. The* DOCTOR *quickly gains control of himself.)*

SANTEE: Say, look Doc, I'm with you in this. I never wanted to let Cody off the hook. I'm with you.

DOCTOR: Yes. I can see that. Fetch my bag.

SANTEE: What?

DOCTOR: My bag!

SANTEE: Yessir. You bet. I'm with you in this.

*(*SANTEE *gets the* DOCTOR's *bag and give it to him.)*

DOCTOR: And stop repeating foolish platitudes. I've grown quite tired of all this trivia. Something drastic must take place.

BEAUJO: Drastic?

DOCTOR: Yes, that's right. Something rather more adventurous. You're a man of adventure aren't you Beaujo?

BEAUJO: Well not exactly. I mean I been around but —

DOCTOR: You've been around?

BEAUJO: Yessir. I mean, the States, you know. I've seen the States.

DOCTOR: I see. Did you discover anything of particular interest in your travels?

BEAUJO: Well, you know, the usual stuff. Card games, pool halls, that kinda' stuff.

DOCTOR: Then you're a man who can recognize gifts.

BEAUJO: Gifts? Well, I don't — I don't exactly get what you mean.

DOCTOR: What I mean very simply is that perhaps in a card game you noticed a particular player who seemed to have more luck that the others. Perhaps even yourself. Something more than luck. A gift we might say.

BEAUJO: Yeah. You might say that.

SANTEE: Say, what's goin' on here anyway?

DOCTOR: Please be silent until you're spoken to!

SANTEE: Yessir.

(During all this the DOCTOR *has placed his black bag on the bed and opened it. As he talks he handles various unseen objects in the bag.)*

DOCTOR: I'm not speaking superstitiously you understand. Luck is no accident. It's a phenomenon. Luck is a living thing. The problem of course is tracking it down.

BEAUJO: Yeah, I see what you mean.

DOCTOR: Do you? You see, in Cody here we had actually tracked it down. We had placed it on the map. We combed the planet for someone like him and we finally found him. In Wyoming of all places.

FINGERS: That's enough Doctor! Enough!

DOCTOR: These dreams, these visions that he has, do you suppose they are purely accident? Mere coincidence?

BEAUJO: Well, I don't know. I couldn't say for sure. Look, I'm just a sidekick here. I don't know anything important.

DOCTOR: Fair enough, but there's no harm in investigating a few details.

BEAUJO: I'd rather you talked to Santee about it. I'm liable to get a headache and go right out on ya!

DOCTOR: Santee has no space between his ears for anything new.

I was hoping perhaps you would.

FINGERS (*still on the floor*): You can't do this! No one's prepared.

DOCTOR: I recognized you immediately, Beaujo, as a man of adventure.

BEAUJO: You did?

DOCTOR: Yes. A man who's been around as you say. A man who's looked life in the face. You have dreams don't you Beaujo?

BEAUJO: Sure. Santee's the only one that don't have dreams.

DOCTOR: What do you dream about?

BEAUJO: Pool mostly. Fast cars. Money.

DOCTOR: Yes. Pool, fast cars and money. Probably women too?

BEAUJO: Sure.

DOCTOR: You can see the difference between your dreams and someone like Cody's. You can recognize that you're worlds apart.

BEAUJO: I guess so. I never thought about it too much.

DOCTOR: Of course not. No reason to think about it. That's my job. I'm the doctor. You're simply the bodyguard.

SANTEE: Could I say somethin' here?

DOCTOR: No! Be quiet! Come here and look in this bag Beaujo. I want you to see something.

FINGERS: NO! Don't look! Don't look Beaujo!

DOCTOR: You are a man of adventure aren't you Beaujo? I wasn't wrong in that was I?

BEAUJO: I'm feelin' a little paralyzed Doc. I don't know what it is. I'm afraid.

DOCTOR: There's nowhere to run to. Besides, it could turn out to be something quite extraordinary. Come have a look.

SANTEE: I'll look.

DOCTOR: Stay where you are! Beaujo?

BEAUJO: What's in it?

DOCTOR: Come and look.

BEAUJO: What if I can't take it. I'm not a very strong person.

DOCTOR: It doesn't matter. Nothing will hurt you. Just come and look in the bag.

(A moment of silence while BEAUJO *decides.* BEAUJO *slowly crosses to the bag where the* DOCTOR *is and looks into it.)*

FINGERS: Oh God. On my God.

BEAUJO: What are they?

DOCTOR: Take one in your hand. Go ahead. Nothing will happen, I promise.
(BEAUJO *reaches into the bag and pulls out a small white bone the size of a large marble. He holds it in the palm of his hand.)*

BEAUJO: What is it?

DOCTOR: A bone from the back of the neck. A dreamer's bone.

BEAUJO: Human?

DOCTOR: Yes.

BEAUJO: You mean you cut it out of somebody?

DOCTOR: In a dreamer's prime he collects certain valuable substances from his dreams in the back of his neck. Even when he loses his touch these substances remain imbedded in these magical bones. A man in possession of enough of these bones becomes eternally linked to the dreamer's magic. His gift lives on.

BEAUJO: You mean these are from dead dreamers?

DOCTOR: I wouldn't say dead exactly. Out of their bodies perhaps but not dead.

BEAUJO: And they help you pick the winners?

DOCTOR: Infallibly.

BEAUJO: Then what's the point in having live dreamers all the time.

DOCTOR: Unfortunately the bones tend to fade in strength. Their power has to continually be replenished. This is where the adventure comes in. It's a very delicate process finding the correct dreamer to restore the power. It has to be one who has experienced a certain stretch of genius. One who is beginning to fade but not to such an extent as to have lost all his magic. Like Cody here for instance. He appears to be the perfect choice.

CODY: Oh no ya' don't. Not me boy. Not this kid. I ain't gettin' cut up and put in no bag. This has gone far enough. I've played ball with you right down the line but this is the limit. No more.

DOCTOR: Santee, strap him to the bed!

SANTEE: With pleasure.

(SANTEE *goes after* CODY. *There's a mad chase around the room.* FINGERS *weeps and moans on the floor. The* DOCTOR *pulls a huge syringe out of his bag.* BEAUJO *is frozen.*)

DOCTOR: You see the territory he travels in. He's perfectly capable of living in several worlds at the same time. This is his genius.

CODY: I was just bluffin'! Honest! I made it all up! I got no magic! I was just pretending!

DOCTOR: Right now he'll do anything to deny his gifts. His gifts are poison to him now. If he knew his power he could even make us disappear. Fortunately he's just a slave for us.

SANTEE: Come here you greaseball! (CODY *keeps getting away from* SANTEE.)

FINGERS: Stop it! You've got to stop it! Beaujo do something!

DOCTOR: You see how we're each on our own territory right now. Each of us paralyzed within certain boundaries. We'd do anything to cross the border but we're stuck. Quite stuck.

BEAUJO: You're gonna operate on him?

DOCTOR: I'm simply going to alter the balance of things. Like a great chef. A pinch of this with a pinch of that. You'd be amazed at how little it takes to create an explosion. Santee, put him on the bed.

(SANTEE *has* CODY *in a firm grip.* CODY *squeals and squirms but* SANTEE *is too strong. He hauls* CODY *over to the bed and throws him down on his back then straddles his stomach and holds his arms down.*)

BEAUJO: Maybe there's some other way. I mean maybe we could hypnotize him or something. I keep putting myself in his place.

DOCTOR: That's quite impossible Beaujo. You see there's no way for you to be in his place. There's no way for any of us to be in any place but the one we're in right now. Each of us. Quite separate from each other and yet connected. It's quite extraordinary isn't it? Now hold him down Santee. It's important to get a direct hit.

(SANTEE *holds* CODY'S *arm and slowly injects the serum.* CODY *becomes calm and speaks very evenly.* BEAUJO *looks on.*)

CODY: The white buffalo. Approach him in a sacred manner. He is

Wakan. The ground he walks is Wakan. This day has sent a
spirit gift. You must take it. Clean your heart of evil
thoughts. Take him in a sacred way. If one bad thought is
creeping in you it will mean your death. You will crumble to
the earth. You will vanish from this time.

DOCTOR: Santee, hand me my scalpel please. It's in my bag.

SANTEE: Sure thing Doc.

(SANTEE *hands the* DOCTOR *a scalpel from out of the bag. A
series of knocks at the door. The* DOCTOR *remains cool.*)

DOCTOR: Beaujo would you mind answering that. It's probably
our waiter.

(BEAUJO *crosses to the door as the* DOCTOR *cuts into the back
of* CODY'S *neck with the scalpel.* CODY *makes no sound.*
BEAUJO *swings the door open. A shotgun blast throws him
clear across the room. He lies in a heap.* CODY'S *two brothers,*
JASPER *and* JASON *enter. They're both about six foot five and
weigh 250 lbs. each. They wear Wyoming cowboy gear with
dust covering them from head to foot. Their costumes should
be well used and authentic without looking like dime-store
cowboys. They both carry double-barrelled twelve-gauge
shotguns and wear side guns on their waists. The* DOCTOR
turns suddenly toward them. Another shotgun blast from
JASPER. *The* DOCTOR *sinks to the floor.* SANTEE *reaches for his
pistol and is cut down by both shotguns at once.* FINGERS
whimpers on the floor. JASPER *and* JASON *look at him stony-
faced.* CODY *sits on the bed with the back of his neck
bleeding. He doesn't know where he is.* JASPER *crosses slowly
over to* FINGERS *with his spurs jangling. He peers down at
him.*)

JASPER: We come fer our brother mister. You so much as make a
twitch and you can kiss tomorrow goodbye.

JASON (*crossing to* CODY): Come on boy. We're goin' home now.

CODY: One bad thought. A clean heart.

JASON (*helping* CODY *to his feet*): Come on now. You gather
yerself together. A little beef stew in yer gullet, you'll be good
as new.

CODY (*standing*): In a sacred way. This day. Sacred. I was
walking in my dream. A great circle. I was walking and I

stopped. Even after the smoke cleared I couldn't see my home. Not even a familiar rock. You could tell me it was anywhere and I'd believe ya'. You could tell me it was any old where.

(JASON leads CODY slowly out the door as JASPER backs out keeping his eye on FINGERS. They disappear out the door. A short pause. The WAITER enters briskly into the room carrying a silver serving tray with three bottles of booze and sparkling glasses. He stops short center stage and looks around the room at all the corpses. His eyes finally fall on FINGERS who moans softly.)

WAITER: Is there something I could get you sir?

FINGERS: The record *(gesturing to the album).* Put the record on.

WAITER: Very good sir.

(The WAITER puts down his tray and picks up the record. He puts it on the record player. The song plays. It is 'Zydeco et pas sale' on Side 2 of 'Clifton Chenier's Very Best', on EMI, Harvest Recordings. The WAITER stands and listens to the tune as the lights fade. The music continues as the audience leaves.)

Operation Sidewinder

A Play in Two Acts

ACT ONE

The houselights come down. The stage is black. The sound of a rattlesnake rattling. A coyote in the distance. The rattle grows louder. A soft blue light fills the ceiling of the stage then flashes off. A bright flash of yellow light from the center of the stage floor then black again. The blue light comes on and goes out. Again the yellow light flashes, then comes on again slowly and glows brightly, with the rest of the stage dark. It forms almost a perfect circle. In the center of the circle can be seen a very large sidewinder rattlesnake, coiled and ready to strike. The light seems to be coming from the snake itself. When stretched to its full length the sidewinder measures over six feet and looks like it weighs over thirty pounds. The eyes are ruby red and blink on and off. The tongue spits. The rattle rattles. The snake's skin is bright yellow with black diamonds. It undulates in a mechanical rhythm. Its hissing grows louder and the rattle too. The head sways from side to side. Sound of a jet going across the sky very loudly, then into silence, then a sonic boom. Silence. Sound of a car passing on a highway. A MAN'S VOICE is heard.

MAN'S VOICE: Look, Honey!
>   *(Sound of car screeching to stop, then backing up, then stopping again. Sound of car door slamming. Bright yellow desert light comes up and fills the stage, making it hard to see the snake except for the black diamonds and the ruby eyes. The snake keeps up its rhythmic rattle, sway, blink, hiss as the MAN enters from stage left with a fancy looking movie camera, straw cowboy hat, open shirt, hairy chest, Bermuda shorts and Hush Puppies. He yells back off left.)*

MAN: Bring the tripod, Honey! Hurry Up!

(He starts focusing his camera on the sidewinder and inching in on it, taking his eye away from the view finder every once in a while to make sure he's not getting too close. HONEY, a very sexy chick with long blonde hair and tight pants, high heels, etc., comes running on from left with a tripod.)

Take it easy! Not so fast! We don't want to get him aggravated.

HONEY: Boy, what a monster! I've never seen one so huge.

(She hands him the tripod. The MAN sets up the camera on the tripod and moves in for a close shot.)

Be careful, Dukie. They're deadly poisonous. I read it in one of those desert manuals. They're the only thing to really be afraid of out here.

MAN: Don't worry. I didn't spend the best part of my years in the Philippines for nothing you know.

(HONEY makes a wide circle around the sidewinder as she talks and the sound of the camera whirring is heard as the MAN shoots. The sidewinder just keeps up his tense rhythm.)

HONEY: He's actually kind of beautiful when you look at him close. I was always taught to be afraid of snakes but actually they're not so bad. I mean he's just out here trying to get a suntan or something. There's nothing awful about that. He looks kind of tense but I'll bet he'd loosen up in no time at all if he got the right kind of attention. You know what I mean, Dukie? Little mice and stuff. I'll bet he'd make a nice pet.

(The MAN straightens up from his camera.)

MAN: Maybe we oughta' aggravate him a little, Honey. He blends right into the background when he's not moving. I don't want to waste any more film than I have to.

HONEY: O.K.

(She stomps her foot and hisses at the sidewinder.)

MAN: Now wait a minute! For crying out loud! Not like that.

HONEY: Well how then?

MAN: Well I don't know. Aren't there some stones around we could throw at him?

HONEY: Nope. Just sand.

MAN: Well how about a stick then?

HONEY: I don't see any.

(Suddenly the sidewinder leaps out and grabs HONEY *around the neck and pulls her to the ground. She screams. The* MAN *jumps and crashes into his camera; it smashes to pieces. He falls on the ground and frantically scrambles away as the snake coils around* HONEY's *body. She screams and kicks but the sidewinder coils tighter so that it's completely wrapped around her from her neck to her feet. The* MAN *watches on his hands and knees as the eyes of the sidewinder blink, the tongue spits and hisses, and the rattle rattles.)*

MAN: Now, Honey, take it easy! Don't fight it. You'll just make him madder than he already is. Just relax and I'll go try to find a Forest Ranger.

HONEY: Oh fuck! He's really got me. Don't leave! Dukie!

MAN: I'll be right back. Try to relax, Honey. Don't make a move until I get back.

(He runs off right.)

BLACKOUT

(The song "Do It Girl" comes on in the blackout. The red eyes of the sidewinder blink in the dark.)

DO IT GIRL

Everytime I see you wanna do it girl
Right out in the street I wanna do it girl
In front of everybody wanna do it girl
I'm losing my control I feel it in my soul

I wanna do it I wanna do it
I wanna do it, do it, do it, do it,
do it, do it, do it, do it, do it

Like a reindeer in the tundra
Wanna do it girl
Like a reptile on a mesa
Wanna do it girl
Like a tiger in the jungle
Wanna do it girl
So lay it on the line
I need you all the time

I wanna do it I wanna do it
I wanna do it, do it, do it, do it,
do it, do it, do it, do it, do it

I know you're going to love the
Way I do it girl
I know you're going to bless the day
I do it girl
There really isn't much to say
But do it girl
The time is going fast, so let the
Good times last

I wanna do it I wanna do it
I wanna do it, do it, do it, do it,
do it, do it, do it, do it, do it

by PETER STAMPFEL & ANTONIA
Music by HOLY MODAL ROUNDERS

SCENE TWO

The song fades out. The blinking red eyes turn to yellow lights and slowly rise about ten feet off the ground. Voices are heard in the dark as the lights fade up and reveal a small Volkswagen in the air on a hydraulic lift with the tail end facing the audience, its yellow tail lights blinking on and off. Below the car is a MECHANIC dressed in greasy coveralls holding a wrench, rag and oil can. Next to him is a YOUNG MAN with long blond hair down to his shoulders, a bright purple T shirt, tight leather pants and bare feet. They are both looking up underneath the car with their backs turned toward the audience as they talk.

MECHANIC: So for no reason at all they just all of a sudden started blinkin' on and off?

YOUNG MAN: Well it seemed like the whole car shook for a second and then they started to blink. All the lights.

MECHANIC: Well, it could be your voltage regulator or the generator. I'll just check out yer wiring here to make sure.

YOUNG MAN: Thanks.

MECHANIC: Could've picked yerself a better time to make a movie ya' know. Days get pretty hot and long this time a' year.

YOUNG MAN: Yeah. I know.

MECHANIC: Even the all year arounders usually leave 'round about now. They migrate around May or June at the latest, then come back toward the tail end of September.

YOUNG MAN: Where do they go?

MECHANIC: Oh, some move into the San Berdoo Valley, some even go to Hollywood, L.A., around in there.

YOUNG MAN: No kidding.

MECHANIC: Yeah. You come here from there and they go there from here. Crazy.

YOUNG MAN: Crazy.

MECHANIC: I suppose what with all the earthquake scares and riots and all there's gonna be a lot more folks movin' out here in the desert.

YOUNG MAN: Yeah. I suppose.

(The MECHANIC *fiddles around with some wires under the car. The* YOUNG MAN *is getting impatient.)*

MECHANIC: Well, you're gettin' paid good for your work so why should you care. How much do you get for a movie anyway?

YOUNG MAN: It depends.

MECHANIC: At least a thousand, right?

YOUNG MAN: At least.

MECHANIC: Where'd you go to College?

YOUNG MAN: I didn't.

MECHANIC: Me neither. I'm in the wrong racket though. You know how many months I gotta work to clear a thousand? Take a guess.

YOUNG MAN: A million months. Look, what about my car? Can I get going pretty soon?

MECHANIC: Sure, sure....

(A pistol falls from under the car onto the ground. The MECHANIC *looks at it then at the* YOUNG MAN. *The* YOUNG MAN *bends down and picks it up.)*

Say, you better hadn't let the Ranger catch you with that thing, son. No firearms allowed in the National Monument.

YOUNG MAN: Oh, it's all right. It's not mine. I'm taking it to a friend of mine who lives on the desert. It's his. I had it cleaned for him and put a new chamber in. He's a prospector so he never gets a chance to come into town much. So I told him I'd do it for him.

MECHANIC: Well I never heard of no prospector using a weapon like that.

(Sound of a car coming up fast and screeching to a stop. The YOUNG MAN tries to hide the gun in his pants but it won't fit so he just sticks his hand inside his shirt with the pistol bulging out. The MAN from the first scene rushes on from stage right.)

MAN: Oh—oh—I need some help. Anyone. You've got to come quick. Help—

MECHANIC: Take her easy there, mister. Catch your breath. I'll get you something to set on.

(The MECHANIC goes off right and comes back with a wooden crate. The MAN is panting and looking at the YOUNG MAN who is getting uptight. The MECHANIC sets down the crate and sits the MAN down.)

Here now. Here. Sit down for a second and get your breath back.

MAN: Oh—you've got to send help.

MECHANIC: What's the problem now?

MAN: My wife. Honey. My wife. She—

YOUNG MAN: What about my car!

MECHANIC: What *about* your wife?

MAN: She's—she's been attacked.

MECHANIC: Attacked?

YOUNG MAN: Come off it.

MAN: By a snake.

MECHANIC: You mean she got bit? Was it a rattler?

MAN: A huge snake.

MECHANIC: Now calm down and try to tell me where she was bit. It's important.

MAN: In the neck. Then—all over. All over.

(The YOUNG MAN whips out the pistol and holds it on the MECHANIC.)

YOUNG MAN: Now stop fucking around and fix my car, you dumb grease monkey!

MECHANIC: Now just a second, kid.

MAN: You've got to help me. My wife's going to die!

(The MAN *becomes hysterical and jumps up from the crate, rushing toward the* YOUNG MAN *who fires the pistol hitting the* MAN *in the stomach and sending him backwards. He lies in a heap, dead. The* MECHANIC *moves toward him. The* YOUNG MAN *stops him with the gun.)*

YOUNG MAN: Hold it! Get my car down off the rack! Hurry up! Get it down!

MECHANIC: You're in some pickle now, son.

YOUNG MAN: Don't say anything. Just get my car down!

MECHANIC: And what if I don't?

YOUNG MAN: Then *I'll* get it down!

(He fires again, hitting the MECHANIC *in the stomach. The* MECHANIC *falls back on top of the* MAN's *body. The* YOUNG MAN *rushes to a lever under the lift and pulls it. Nothing happens. He yanks it to the right and left. Nothing happens. He kicks the lever. Still nothing.)*

YOUNG MAN: Come on, come on! Work, mother fucker! Work! Why won't you work! Work! Please work! Please! Pretty please! Work. Oh work! Please work! Work! Work! Work! Work! Work!

(Sound of bell in gas station and car pulling up and stopping off left. The YOUNG MAN *runs off right leaving the car up on the rack. Sound of jet passing overhead. Silence. A man is heard whistling off left.)*

VOICE: Shorty! Anybody home?

(A FOREST RANGER *comes on from left, dressed in uniform and sipping a Coke. He just wanders onstage without seeing the bodies and glancing up at the car.)*

BLACKOUT

("Pipeline" by the HOLY MODAL ROUNDERS *comes on in the dark.)*

FLOAT ME DOWN YOUR PIPELINE

Float me down your pipeline sometime
I came here with my guidebook
With my license in hand

But the landing field keeps slipping out of line
And this ain't what they told me I'd find
The biggest laugh around here
Is the changing ground here
Down in the alley
When the game gets fast
There ain't no piece of paper
Gonna save your ass
So float me down your pipeline sometime

I need to find a guideline sometime
These old concentric circles
Are spinning me out
And everything I do goes down in doubt
So won't you show me which way is out
I guess this is the moment
When I might need a friend
Backwater waiting for my mind to break
Guess you're the only chance that's left to take
So float me down your pipeline sometime.

by ANTONIA
Music by HOLY MODAL ROUNDERS

SCENE THREE

The song fades into the sound of the sidewinder's rattle. The blinking red eyes are seen in the dark. The lights come up on BILLY, *an old prospector with a long gray beard, floppy hat, yellow shirt, red bandana, overalls with suspenders, long boots, pots and pans attached to his waist so they clang when he walks, and a pack on the floor beside him. He is sitting on his haunches directly behind* HONEY *who is lying frozen in the same position with the snake coiled around her body.* BILLY *talks to her in a calm soothing voice. The snake continues its rhythms.*

BILLY: Well, that was just about nineteen-o-six when they was a' gettin' all het up about the area. Yep. If you'd a told any one a' them ten thousand folks back then that their boom town weren't a gonna have nothin' left but a shanty and some wild burros come nineteen—seventy-one, why there wouldn't a' been a one of 'em would a paid ya' no never mind. No sir. They smelled that gold pumpin' through the rhyolite and there weren't no one gonna stop that town from boomin'. 'Course there's still a few old tough ones like myself and Death Valley Smiley and Wheelburro Tex and Dapper Tommy Thompson and some a the others. Still loco enough to believe them old yarns.

(HONEY *makes a low groaning sound and starts to undulate with the sidewinder. She seems to get more and more turned on as* BILLY *tries to calm her.*)

BILLY: Now, ya' don't want to move around much there, Miss. I've seen these here critters strike so fast it'd make yer head swim. 'Course now this one's a bit extra sized. Can't say fer certain when I ever did see such a big one. If it weren't the middle of the American desert here I'd even be prone to say she was a boa constrictor. Like they have in Africa and such. 'Course that's a tad far fetched. Never can tell though. Them Air Force boys pull some mighty funny stunts out here. There's a bunch of 'em stationed just close by here ya' know. Over at Fort George. Maybe you seen 'em roarin' by. Roarin' by. Testin' the sky fer holes or somethin'. Nothin' else to do. Could be one a them fellas dropped this big feller right out a' the sky. Ain't likely. I mean, first off they'd have to fly off to Africa to get the damned thing in the first place. Then fly it back out here. Ain't likely. Could just be though. They get so galldarned bored I'll betcha'. Testin' all the time. Sure. Nothin' else to do but fly around makin' explosions. Droppin' snakes. Probably think it's funny. Get a big charge outa' trappin' young ladies. I'll betcha'.

(HONEY *has an orgasm as the* YOUNG MAN *comes running on from right.* BILLY *smiles and stands up, his arms outstretched. The* YOUNG MAN *crosses down left paying no attention to* HONEY *or the sidewinder.*)

BILLY: Jimmy boy! Right on time. Just like clock work. Look what I found here, Danny. Just lyin' here while I was a waitin'. Come by to wait and here she was, all bound up and chokin' to death. So I tried to tell her a thing or two about the desert and snakes and such.

YOUNG MAN: Come here, Billy.

BILLY: What ya' got there, Johnny? I been a' waitin' like ya' told me. I don't ferget.

(BILLY *crosses down to the* YOUNG MAN *who takes out the gun and runs his hands over it. The* YOUNG MAN *turns to* BILLY *and holds out the gun for him to see.* BILLY *takes it.)*

BILLY: Oh, now Jimmy, ya' shore got a nice one. Ya' needn't a' got such a nice rod fer that half breed. He don't know the difference 'tween a B.B. gun and a thirty-odd-six.

YOUNG MAN: I want him to have this one. You'll see that he gets it, Billy?

BILLY: Shore. I'll hand it right over. No trouble 'tall.

YOUNG MAN: Now listen carefully. I've run into some trouble so I'm going to have to do some doubling back. Now tell Mickey Free to meet me right here tomorrow at sunrise. You got that?

BILLY: Sunrise tomorrow.

YOUNG MAN: Right. Now tell him to come alone and not to bring the gun. I'll explain the rest when he gets here.

BILLY: Alone and no iron. I savvy, Johnny.

YOUNG MAN: O.K. Now get going.

BILLY: What about the lady?

YOUNG MAN: What lady?

(BILLY *motions to* HONEY *who again has become rigid as the sidewinder blinks and spits and rattles.)*

She's got nothing to do with me. Now get going and remember what I just told you.

BILLY: O.K., Danny. Adios!

(*The* YOUNG MAN *hurries off right.* BILLY *walks up to* HONEY *and around behind her. He picks up his pack and slings it over his shoulder. He bends over and looks into* HONEY's *face. Her eyes are into a blank stare.* BILLY *shakes his head and goes off left twirling the pistol and singing softly.)*

"A beautiful bird in a gilded cage.
A beautiful sight to see.
You may think she's happy and free from fear.
She ain't though she seems to be."

(*The lights fade to* BLACKOUT *as* BILLY *exits.*)

(*"Generalonely" is heard in the* BLACKOUT.)

GENERALONELY
Sad news has come to town, the blues it came in
Right up through my front door, looked like it was staying
My aide de camp replied, "What's that it's saying"
The blues has come to town looks like it's staying

A General am I and a General only
Generally I'm generally lonely
A General am I and a General only
Generally I'm generally lonely

Generally I'm generally lonely
Generally but a General only
Then my aide de camp replied, "The legal tenderly
And now we are all registered blues members"

by STEVE WEBER
Music by HOLY MODEL ROUNDERS

SCENE FOUR

The song fades out as the lights come up on an Air Force
COLONEL *seated behind his desk with a glass of brandy and a
cigar, his foot up on his desk. Across from him is a* CAPTAIN, *also
sipping brandy but slightly drunker than the* COLONEL. *Behind
them is a huge colorful map of the U.S. American eagle.
Photographs of jets in flight. Trophies on the desk.*

COLONEL: Trouble with that bitch was, you just didn't get her out in the world enough, Henry. A young bitch like that's gotta come in contact with a whole lotta people and noise. Otherwise you'll just never get her cured. There's a world of difference between your dog and your bitch. A lot of breeders forget that. Just like people. Now a woman's just naturally gonna' be more sensitive than a man. No two ways about it. Same with a dog.

CAPTAIN: I don't know about that, Warner. I've seen some pretty spookey males in my day.

COLONEL: Sure! You're gonna get your share of gun shy males too. No way around it. That's that old argument. That heredity and environment thing. I wouldn't be the one to take sides for either. They both got their strong points. But I'll tell you this much. You can't expect a young pup, male or female, to grow up into a healthy bird dog if he's had a bad surrounding when he was little. Like a pup who's been around a lot of little brats pestering him all the time and making loud noises right in his ear. He's not gonna grow up as brave as the pup who had a quiet peaceful home. Have some more brandy, Henry.

CAPTAIN: No. No thanks.

COLONEL: Aw, go on. Don't cost me nothin'.

CAPTAIN: All right.

(The COLONEL *pours him another drink.)*

Say, Warner, you know that big stud dog you got? The one with the speckled chest?

COLONEL: Bruce. Sure. Oh no. I'm reading your mind right now, Captain.

CAPTAIN: What?

COLONEL: I suppose you want to breed that gun shy bitch of yours to my male.

CAPTAIN: Well her conformation makes up for her temperment. You gotta admit that much. She's got one of the best heads you'll see in a long time.

COLONEL: A pretty head don't mean she can smell birds. Some of the best hunting dogs I've seen have been ugly as sin. Now come on, Henry. You don't want my Bruce to go getting a trauma right off the bat. He's only sired two litters so far, and if she gives him a bad bite he might never get over it. I mean I gotta think of his future too.

CAPTAIN: She's not gonna go biting your male, Warner. Besides, we could muzzle her.

COLONEL: Oh no. Absolutely not! I never muzzled a dog in my life and I never will. I don't care if it's the meanest dog around. That's something you just don't do to an animal. I saw a dog almost suffocate on its own saliva once. Just from that very same thing.

CAPTAIN: Well we wouldn't go off and leave them alone. I'd stand right there and hold her.

COLONEL: I'm sorry, Henry. It's just not the way I like to breed my dogs. It's a very touchy game. You're dealing with living animals, not machines.

(A loud knock on the door.)

Come in!

(A CADET enters and salutes stiffly.)

At ease.

CADET: Colonel, sir. Your presence is requested immediately at the laboratory, sir. It seems the sidewinder computer has escaped.

(The COLONEL stands abruptly, knocking over his brandy glass. The CAPTAIN tries to get out of his seat but he's too drunk.)

COLONEL: Escaped! What do you mean escaped! It's under strict surveillance!

CADET: I'm not sure, sir. That was the message from General Browser, sir.

COLONEL: How could a computer escape? Answer me that!

CADET: I have no idea, sir. That was the whole message, sir. General Browser and Dr. Vector are waiting in the lab, sir.

COLONEL: Tell them I'm on my way. Go on!

CADET: Yes sir!

(The CADET salutes and exits.)

COLONEL: Of all the goddamned nerve! Escaped!

BLACKOUT

("Catch Me" comes on in the dark.)

CATCH ME

Catch me if you can while I last 'cause there's nothin' to
    keep me around
Touch me with a ten foot pole and I'll make both your feet
    leave the ground
Watch me if you can't come along 'cause I got enough here
    for us both
It's eating me inside out but I know that it won't stunt my
    growth

It doesn't matter what you try it's all about take and give
It doesn't matter how you die but only how you live

I'm burning up ninety-nine pounds of rubber up here in the
    sky
I don't know just how I got wheels or why it's so easy to fly
I can't see for millions of miles it looks like a fog up ahead
Catch me if I crash to the ground and make sure I don't land
    on my head

It doesn't matter what you try it's all about take and give
It doesn't matter how you die but only how you live

by SAM SHEPARD
Music by HOLY MODAL ROUNDERS

SCENE FIVE

*(The song fades into the rattle of the sidewinder. The blinking
red eyes. Hissing. The lights come up on HONEY, still entangled by
the sidewinder. Three men are standing behind her, watching the
sidewinder intently. MICKEY FREE is in the middle with two*

Apache INDIANS *standing slightly behind him, on either side. All three have long flowing black hair which falls down over their shoulders. The two* INDIANS *are very dark skinned and dressed in the renegade Apache costume of the late eighteen hundreds, but unique from each other. Knee length moccasin boots, rawhide pants, long loin cloths with Mexican type designs, heavy shirts, suit jackets captured from wayward whites, tooth and bone necklaces, straight brimmed black hats with Mexican silver coin headbands, two wide belts of ammunition criss-crossing from shoulder to waist, knives sticking out of the tops of their moccasins and 30.30 rifles from the cavalry times.* MICKEY FREE *is a half breed: Mexican, Irish, Apache; his skin is lighter but he looks Indian. He's half blind in his right eye so he squints it constantly and moves his head in strange ways. He is dressed like the Apaches but flashier in spots and more heavily armed. His prize weapon is a huge Bowie knife with a turquoise and silver handle which he keeps in a beaded deerskin sheath which hangs down over his crotch, like a cock piece. All three of them watch* HONEY *and the sidewinder in silence as she goes through throes of agony-ecstasy with the sidewinder continuing his relentless moves and rhythms. Finally her eyes open and she looks up at* MICKEY FREE.

HONEY: Help me.

> *(The* INDIANS *are silent.* MICKEY FREE *stares at her with his one good eye.)*
> Please. Help me.
> *(*MICKEY *turns to the* INDIANS. *The* INDIANS *speak to him in Apache. The language should sound like a mixture of Spanish and Oriental.)*

1ST INDIAN: Natcha la oot. Gracha om laate.

2ND INDIAN: No me ta santo. Esta un gran mal muerta.

> *(*MICKEY FREE *is silent. He turns back to* HONEY *and looks down at her.)*

HONEY: Please, help me. Please. Help me.

> *(*MICKEY *takes out his huge Bowie knife and kneels down beside* HONEY. *He strokes the head of the sidewinder with his left hand very gently and makes a soothing sound in his throat. Suddenly his left hand seizes the neck of the*

sidewinder and squeezes it. The jaws pop open revealing huge fangs. He makes one sudden slash with the knife and the head comes off, leaving the body writhing and squirming on HONEY, *who screams and goes into hysteria. She flings the body downstage and collapses. The body writhes as* MICKEY *slowly stands up still holding the head with eyes still blinking. The* INDIANS *make sounds of approval and touch the snake's head.* MICKEY *smiles and wipes the knife off on his pants then puts it back in the sheath. He drops the head into a beaded pouch which he wears on his waist. The body stops writhing. The* VOICE *of the* YOUNG MAN *is heard off right.)*

YOUNG MAN'S VOICE: Mickey? That you, Mickey?

(MICKEY *and the* INDIANS *look off right.* HONEY *is in delirium daze.)*

HONEY: Dukie?

(The YOUNG MAN *comes on from right.)*

YOUNG MAN: Mickey! You made it!

I see you're free now. Why don't you split.

(HONEY *looks bewildered. The* YOUNG MAN *moves center downstage,* MICKEY *follows with the* INDIANS *close behind. The* YOUNG MAN *takes two plasticene bags filled with white powder out of his crotch and sets them on the ground. He sits down cross-legged.* MICKEY *sits beside him with the bags between them. The* INDIANS *stand behind.)*

YOUNG MAN: Did Billy give you the gun?

MICKEY: Yes.

YOUNG MAN: Is it all right?

MICKEY: Yes.

YOUNG MAN: Good. Now—

MICKEY: I'll need more than one gun.

YOUNG MAN: O.K. I'll see what I can do. How many do you want?

MICKEY: Two more.

YOUNG MAN: O.K. I'll get them by next week. How's that?

MICKEY: Good. Give them to Billy.

YOUNG MAN: Yeah. Now ....

MICKEY: You have a ready roll?

YOUNG MAN: Sure.

(*He takes out a cigarette and hands it to* MICKEY.)

MICKEY: You have two more?

(*The* YOUNG MAN *offers the pack to the two* INDIANS.)

YOUNG MAN: Here. Keep the pack.

(*The* INDIANS *take the pack and take out cigarettes.* MICKEY *puts out his hand to the* INDIANS. *They give the pack to* MICKEY *who puts it in the top of his moccasin.* MICKEY *takes out a butane lighter from his other moccasin and lights his cigarette, then he lights the* INDIANS'.)

YOUNG MAN: Now, this is the stuff. It's more than enough to do the trick.

MICKEY: Trick?

YOUNG MAN: Yeah. Trick, job.

MICKEY: Job.

YOUNG MAN: Now your job is very easy but you have to pull it off without fail. There's a lot of people counting on you. People you've never seen before. You're going to mean a lot to them if everything works the way we have it run down. Now the reason we've come to you is because you know the layout of Fort George probably better than anyone in the desert, mainly because you helped them get it started.

MICKEY: Yes. I find them low ground.

YOUNG MAN: Right. And that's valuable to us because now you can take these bags directly to their reservoir and dump them without anyone getting suspicious. Now here's the plan: tomorrow, you and your friends ride into the fort at high noon. You go straight to the commanding officer's headquarters and ask to speak to General Browser. They'll ask you what you want to see him about and you tell them that you're looking for work.

MICKEY: Work!

YOUNG MAN: Yeah. Work, job. You need a job. And then they'll tell you they're very sorry but they have no work, come back some other time, and you say all right and start to leave. Then you ask them if it's all right if you water your horses out at the reservoir because you've been riding all day and they're really wiped out. Then they'll probably give you a pass to enter the reservoir area. If they don't then ask them for one. Then you take the pass, get back on your horses, with the dope in your saddle bags.

MICKEY: Dope?

YOUNG MAN: Yeah, the stuff! And ride into the reservoir area. I doubt if they'll have a guard on duty there but if they do I'm sure you can handle him. Just show him the pass and play dumb. When you get to the reservoir, dismount and water your horses. Then just take the dope out of the saddle bags and cut the bags open and let all the powder fall into the water. Be sure to put the empty plastic bags in your saddle bags. Don't leave them at the reservoir. Then just get back on your horse and ride away. You got it?

MICKEY: Yes.

YOUNG MAN: Good.

MICKEY: I have more friends who wish to help too. They say anything that will make the silver birds leave the skies will be pleasing to the Spider Woman.

YOUNG MAN: Tell them to wait. Anything can happen. We'll let them know.

(MICKEY *gives an order to the* INDIANS.)

MICKEY: Nanza nienta paz. Para los caballos.

(*The* INDIANS *go to the plasticene bags. One of them has a leather saddle bag which he opens while the other one puts the bags inside.* MICKEY *stands up with the* YOUNG MAN. *They shake hands by clasping each other's wrists.*)

YOUNG MAN: I'll come to your place next week and let you know how things went.

MICKEY: Good.

YOUNG MAN: Good luck.

MICKEY: Hasta luego.

(*The three of them go offstage left. The* YOUNG MAN *looks at* HONEY *who is staring at him with a blank gaze.*)

YOUNG MAN: What're you looking at?

(*He reaches into his pocket and pulls out a small leather pouch with a zipper. He sits down and zips it open. He takes out a needle, an eye dropper syringe and a small vial of liquid. He lifts up his T shirt and feels for his belt. He notices he's not wearing one.*)

Hey! Do you have a belt on you? Or a tie?

HONEY: Belt? No.

(*He looks around the stage angrily. He sees the sidewinder's body. He reaches for it and grabs the rattle end, pulling it close to him. He fixes up the needle, opens the vial and draws the liquid up into the syringe.*)

Do you have any water?

YOUNG MAN: Yeah. It's in the canteen.

(HONEY *scrambles to the canteen, opens it and takes a long drink. The* YOUNG MAN *struggles with the snake's body, trying to tie it as a tourniquet around his left arm.*)

HONEY: What are you doing?

YOUNG MAN: Trying to get off. What does it look like. Fuck! Would you come here for a second.

HONEY: What?

YOUNG MAN: Just come here. I'm not going to bite you.

(HONEY *crawls to him on her hands and knees.*)

Would you wrap this tight around my arm and just hold it.

HONEY: Are you crazy? That thing almost strangled me to death.

YOUNG MAN: Well now it's your turn to strangle it. Come on. Look. He's dead.

(*He shakes the sidewinder's body in her face. She jumps back.*)

Dead! Just do it for a favor. O.K.? Please? Come on. Be a sport.

(*She takes the snake and wraps it around his left arm.*)

Pull. Now just hold on to it. Don't let go.

(HONEY *pulls the snake tight. The* YOUNG MAN *rubs his vein and jabs the needle in.* HONEY *makes a shriek and jumps back, letting the snake go. The* YOUNG MAN *lets out a yell.*)

Oh fuck! You stupid cunt! You almost broke my point! My last point! You almost ripped out my vein! Jesus Christ!

(*He rubs his arm in agony.*)

HONEY: I'm sorry. I didn't know you were gonna poke yourself.

YOUNG MAN: I told you not to let go. Now would you wrap it tight and hold on this time.

HONEY: All right.

(*She goes through the same thing again with the snake. He jabs the needle in this time and gets a hit.*)

YOUNG MAN: All right. Now let go slowly. Slowly. Easy. That's it.

(She slowly releases her grip on the sidewinder. It falls to the floor. The YOUNG MAN *relaxes and smiles at* HONEY.)

Now. That wasn't so bad, was it?

HONEY: Are you a diabetic?

YOUNG MAN: Yeah. I need lots of sugar.

HONEY: Could I have some?

YOUNG MAN: You think you need it?

HONEY: I can't seem to get up any energy. I mean you use it for energy, don't you? That darn snake knocked the wind out of me.

YOUNG MAN: I suppose I could spare some. Just to get you up on your feet. Don't come asking me for more though.

HONEY: Oh, I won't. I just need a boost. Boy, I'm really glad you came along. You know? I thought I was gonna be stuck out here forever. There's a lot of creepy people out here. You're the first decent person I've seen.

(He wraps the snake around her right arm.)

YOUNG MAN: All right. Now grab both ends and pull tight. Close your eyes and don't look. O.K.?

(She follows his orders as the YOUNG MAN *fills the syringe and* HONEY *talks with her eyes closed. The lights fade out to* BLACK *as the* YOUNG MAN *shoots her up.)*

HONEY: It's not going to hurt, is it? I've had enough pain for one day. I just have to get up enough energy to look for Dukie. He's my husband. He just all of a sudden ran off some place to get some help and I haven't seen him since. We were on our way to Las Vegas to get a divorce. It's not that we weren't happy or anything. We were very happy. We just needed a change you know. A sort of vacation from each other. So we decided to make it a vacation together. You know what I mean. I mean so long as we were getting divorced we might as well make it a vacation. Kill two birds with one stone. Then this snake got me and I don't even know what happened. One minute we were together and the next minute we were separated. Just like that. I guess this desert does funny things to your brain or something. It's not going to hurt me, is it?

BLACKOUT

(HONEY *screams. "Euphoria" is heard in the dark.)*

EUPHORIA

Ma's out here switchin' in the kitchen
And dad's in the living room grousin' and a bitchin'
And I'm out here kicking the gong for "Euphoria"

Euphoria when your mind goes wheelin' and a walkin'
Your inside voices go squealin' and a squawkin'
Floating around on a belladonna cloud
Singing Euphoria

There's a man in the corner underneath a table
He sat makin' faces at a union label
He pitched his ears and then he rolled his eyes
And whispered "Euphoria"

Euphoria when your mind goes wheelin' and a walkin'
Your inside voices go squealin' and a squawkin'
Floating around on a belladonna cloud
Singing Euphoria

I went for a walk and just got back
I saw a junkie mother boosting Similac
She had her baby on her back and her works in her hand
She hollered "Euphoria"

Euphoria when your mind goes wheelin' and a walkin'
Your inside voices go squealin' and a squawkin'
Floating around on a belladonna cloud
Singing Euphoria

Pinched Eve on the bottom, patted Adam on the back
Smiled at the serpent and it winked back
Took a bite from the apple with two bites gone
And hollered "Euphoria "

Euphoria when your mind goes wheelin' and a walkin'
Your inside voices go squealin' and a squawkin'
Floating around on a belladonna cloud
Singing Euphoria

by ROBIN REMAILY
Copyright—Windfall Music 1968

Music by HOLY MODAL ROUNDERS

SCENE SIX

*The song fades out. The lights slowly come up on a '57 chevy
convertible. Three Blacks are sitting in the car.* BLOOD *is driving.*
BLADE *and* DUDE *sit in the back. Above them hanging in mid air is
a huge hot dog sign. A* CARHOP *enters from left and walks up to the
car. She is young and dressed in a stupid white mini outfit with a
funny hat, a check book and pencil.*

CARHOP: Can I help you guys?

BLOOD (*To the two in back.*): What do you want?

BLADE: Let me have a cheeseburger, a chocolate malt and a order a
fries.

DUDE: Yeah. Same thing for me except make it vanilla.

CARHOP: The malt?

BLOOD: Right.

CARHOP: Say, are you guys with the Panthers?

DUDE: No, we're with the Rams.

BLOOD: Let me have a B.L.T. on whole wheat toast with mayo.

CARHOP: A B.L.T. on whole wheat.

BLOOD: And a large milk.

CARHOP: Sure. You know I've been wanting to talk to some of your
people for a long time. I go to City College and it seems like
there's this whole gap in dialogue between what we're trying
to do and what you're trying to do. You know what I mean?

Like I can really dig this whole unity thing that you guys are into but it seems like we could be doing something to help bind it all together. You know. I mean you people have such a groovy thing going.

BLOOD: Yeah, right.

CARHOP: I mean all this shit about the pigs man. I mean fuck the pigs. Forget all those gray people. We're not going to turn on any of those zombies. We gotta find our own people. Turn ourselves on. Make something happen for us.

DUDE: For us?

CARHOP: Yeah, us. You and me. Fuck them. All that festering bullshit is just going to collapse anyway. I mean I gotta work to pay for my school but once that's over man, I'm gone. You know? I mean I'm going to go out and help organize, help get it together. Because if we don't get it together pretty soon we're gonna be had. Am I right?

BLADE: Right.

CARHOP: And I'm not just doing a rap to make myself feel good either. Because I got nothing to lose. Least of all this shitty job. I mean I can see where things are at. With you guys it's all laid out. With me it's different. I got a lot of guessing to do. With you it's armed struggle. I'm for that. I think it's a necessary step. A revolution begins when a faction seizes power and begins to use it to change society. Armed struggle comes before the revolution. Armed struggle begins when the oppressed people pick up guns and are willing to die for the revolution. I'm willing. I know you guys are. I got a gun right in my house man and I'm ready to use it too.

BLOOD: Good. What kind is it?

CARHOP: What? The gun? I'm not sure. A thirty-eight or something. But listen, we can't afford to compromise anymore. Some people are saying all they want is a piece of the American pie. Well we can't have a piece of that pie because that pie exploits our brothers in Vietnam, in Latin America and in Africa.

BLOOD: Let me have a piece of cherry pie with that too.

CARHOP: Cherry pie?

BLOOD: Yeah. With the B.L.T.

CARHOP: Oh. O.K. All right. One cherry pie. Right. I'll be right back.

(*She writes it down on her check book and exits right.*)

BLOOD: Now, down to business.

DUDE: Yeah, what's the story with this flower child in the desert? You really trust him to deliver the goods?

BLOOD: Don't worry, once that dope takes hold the Air Force is going to be doing some mighty funny things.

BLADE: How's it supposed to work anyway?

BLOOD: Mickey Free makes the drop. Right?

BLADE: Right.

BLOOD: The pilots get a good taste of supersonic water. They start feeling funny. They hear voices. They see things in the air. They hear music. They get stoned like they never been before in their lives.

DUDE: Then what?

BLOOD: In the middle of the night they all get up in unison like Dracula and his sisters and walk straight out into the night. They climb into their sleek super duper F-one-elevens and take off. They fly straight for a little island just south of Miami whereupon they land and await further instructions.

DUDE: Sounds pretty shaky to me.

BLOOD: How come?

DUDE: I don't know, it's just like James Bond or something. Why don't we just go in and take the thing over.

BLADE: Yeah, I can't see getting involved with this hippie cat Blood. His mind's been burned out. The drug thing just isn't going to pull it off.

BLOOD: We gotta give it some time. It's just a step.

DUDE: Watch it, here comes the S.D.S. (*The* CARHOP *enters again with their order. She walks up to them.*)

CARHOP: Say listen I'm sorry I got so carried away before but I really meant what I said.

BLOOD: Right. You got the milk?

CARHOP: Milk? Oh. Yeah. Here it is. I mean we can't debate whether we want revolution or whether we don't want revolution because for our survival we're going to have to make revolution. Right? I mean I guess you guys already know that.

BLADE: Pass the french fries.

BLACKOUT

("Synergy" is heard.)

SYNERGY

CHORUS:

Superman's on the can contemplating synergy
Lone ranger on the range and Dr. Strange got synergy
Cool heads certainly agree concerning synergy
Likewise Liberace's momma
Donald Duck and Dalai Lama
Yes sir!

Come along, sing with me sing a song of synergy
Find that peace in your soul
We're all one and heaven is our goal

CHORUS

Synergy will get us all and it's going to be a ball
Kick that gong, ring that bell, synergy will save us all from
hell

CHORUS

Be a friend, lend a hand, try your best to understand
We are all born alone, but the light of love can lead us home

CHORUS

Get undressed, plant a tree, make love to machinery
Throw away all the locks, open up the jails and stop the
clocks

CHORUS

We can have paradise right now at a bargain price
Heaven is ours to make, peace on earth is there for us to take

CHORUS

by PETER STAMPFEL & ANTONIA
music by HOLY MODAL ROUNDERS

SCENE SEVEN

The Air Force Laboratory at Fort George. Test tubes, vials, bunsen burners, a general clutter of chemical and electronic gadgets. In the middle of all this is DOCTOR VECTOR, *sitting in a wheelchair, dressed in a white chemist's smock. He is very tiny and his entire body is twisted and bent. He wears extra thick dark glasses and elevator shoes and speaks with a weird shifting accent. When he wants to move his wheelchair he presses a button on one of the arms and the chair propels itself electronically. On either side of him are* GENERAL BROWSER, obviously pissed off but trying to keep his cool, *and* COLONEL WARNER *who goes into fits of temper but snaps out of it by the* GENERAL's *presence.*

COLONEL: I've never in my whole career in the United States Air Force heard of such a half cocked idea as this one! I mean freedom to experiment to my mind has always meant for the experimenter, I mean the person or persons doing the experiment, not the goddamn experiment itself! Now that's just never ever been done before, Doctor Vector, and I for one....

GENERAL: Now settle down, Warner. I'm sure the doctor had his reasons for allowing this to happen. What's done is done. The fact is that I should have personally seen to it that the arrangements for Operation Sidewinder were made more clear to everyone involved. Including myself. I certainly had no idea you were off on a tangent like this, Doctor Vector.

DR. VECTOR: What tangent? No tangent. This now is marking the beginning of the stage I had so long awaited. You should both be beaming with the joy I now feel. The sidewinder computer has now chosen to go off on its own accord. It has chosen to be free and exist on its own. For weeks I have watched it writhing and squirming with its wonderful powerful body. Sidewinding its way around its little artificial desert. Searching for a way out. Searching every corner. Its magnificent head straining toward the top of the glass then back down to the bottom. Knowing that all around, outside, out in the real world was a desert and sky so vast and so free. A captive with more cosmic secrets than a man could learn from the whole of history. Finally I saw the decision lay in my hands, gentlemen. In my hands. It was up to me to either keep this creature in its cage and continue to feed it my steady diet of limited knowledge or to set it free and have it discover its true potential. Do you realize the magnitude of this action? It means for the first time ever we can begin to study the effects of the machine's own decisions on its own survival. For the first time in history we shall see if it is possible to produce a machine with its own brain and its own synthetic form of life and have it survive on its own without our constant presence and supervision. All this and still have it retain the willingness to achieve the purpose for which it was programmed. Oh sure, you say it's already been done before. Some biochemist in New Jersey might maybe come up with some small germ of plastic bacteria that he says is life. All year they watch it under glass and give it injections and change the light and switch around the soils but so what! That is no experiment! Not like the sidewinder! The sidewinder computer this very minute is surviving on one of the most inhospitable deserts in the world! Surviving by its own synthetic wits! And you two talk as though we have thrown away a lifetime! Bah! The Army should never have nothing to do with Science!

COLONEL: This is the Air Force, Doctor! And it's not a lifetime that you've thrown away but almost two billion dollars! How does that grab you?

GENERAL: Now wait a minute, Colonel. The Doctor seems to feel that his sidewinder computer will perform better and reveal more information to us if left on its own. That's all well and good. However, I'm left with certain uncertainties, Doctor.

DR. VECTOR: Yah, General?

GENERAL: From a purely pragmatic point of view, now that the computer has escaped, or in your words ventured off on its own, how is it possible for you to program it or even trace its existence, if in fact it is still alive. I mean....

COLONEL: Alive! Judas Priest!

DR. VECTOR: Gentlemen, gentlemen! Operation Sidewinder was begun by the government in late 1964 Yah? (Yah!) in an effort to produce a tracing computer which would help to solve the questions of whether or not unidentified flying objects actually existed. Oui? (Oui!) Since that time we have discovered that they do in fact exist Dah? (Dah!) and the next step, as you both are well aware, was of course to trace their flight patterns in an effort to learn their trade routes and possibly the planet or star from where they are living.

COLONEL: Now come off it, Doc. We all know that Constellation Pegasus has....

GENERAL: Please, Colonel! Let the Doctor finish.

DR. VECTOR: At this stage it became apparent to me that all man made efforts to produce this type of information were useless and that a much more sophisticated form of intelligence was necessary. A form of intelligence which, being triggered from the mind of man, would eventually, if allowed to exist on its own, transcend the barriers of human thought and penetrate an extraterrestrial consciousness. This is when I began my studies of the Western rattlesnakes and experimenting with the possibilities of their rhythmic movements being directly connected with the movements of the planets and the flight patterns of the UFO's. These studies resulted in the initial design for my sidewinder computer. Now, whether or not the sidewinder will be able to attain this realm of extraterrestrial consciousness is something none of us will know until we are ready. One thing is for certain, the sidewinder must have complete freedom to discover this realm for itself. And gentlemen, if it succeeds we will be the first to know. Think of it, gentlemen! We will be in direct contact with these flying objects and eventually with those who operate and control them!

COLONEL: What a bunch a' horse shit.

BLACKOUT

(*"Dusty Fustchuns" comes on in the dark.*)

"DUSTY FUSTCHUNS"

Don't leave me dying in the desert
Don't leave me dangling in the dust
I don't wanna live here with these here lizards
They look at me with a cold and hungry lust
Big bird circlin' in the sky is a buzzard
Think he got his eye on me
The ever shiftin sand is the only sound I hear
And that mirage over there is the only water near

I got a pound of sand in my navel
When night comes I turn into ice
At high noon brains melt like butter
No one to talk to but the toads and the mice

Devil take away these damn sand dunes
Devil take away this sun
Devil take away this dry dusty hole
This is all a mistake and
I'm cooked 'til overdone

(*Coyote howls for last verse*)

by **ROBIN REMAILY**
Music by **HOLY MODAL ROUNDERS**

SCENE EIGHT

The song fades into the sound of crickets. A coyote howls. A full moon glows in the dark. Stars come out. The lights fade up slowly to bluish moonlight. The YOUNG MAN *and* HONEY *are lying on their backs upstage staring at the night sky. The body of the sidewinder is downstage left.* HONEY *moves voluptuously around on her back, stretching and unbuttoning her blouse. The* YOUNG MAN *just stares at the sky.*

HONEY: Oh, it's so gorgeous. A full moon. And the stars. I never felt so good in my whole life. Everything smells so wild out here. Smell the yucca. It's so peaceful and nice. Hey, what's your name anyway? Do you have a name? My name's Honey. That's because my husband called me that. He said it was because of my honey hair. My yellow honey hair. Dukie said it even smelled like honey. You wanna' smell my hair? You can smell it if you want. Sometimes I even smell it. I used to all the time. When I was a little girl. I'd go in the closet and smell it. I never cut it because my Mama said that sometime... someday I'd make my living from my hair. That's what she told me. That I should come to Hollywood and the very next day, just from walking around the streets and everything, that someone would see my hair and ask me to come and get a screen test. And that before very long I'd be famous and rich and everything. I'd never have to worry about a man supporting me or anything because I'd have enough to support myself. And then I met Dukie and....
(A shock of blue light goes off above the stage, like a huge flash bulb. Then a beam of white light goes across the sky behind them from left to right and disappears. HONEY *sits up. The* YOUNG MAN *stays relaxed on his back.* HONEY *stares up at the sky.)*
HONEY: Hey! Did you see that!
YOUNG MAN: Shooting stars.
HONEY: Boy. I never saw one before. It looks like it's still there.

YOUNG MAN: Why should it go away?

HONEY: Well, don't they just fall and then . . . Look! Look at the way it's moving. Sideways. I'm scared.

YOUNG MAN: Why be scared of a star?

HONEY: What if it's not a star? What if it's one of those creepy saucer things?

YOUNG MAN: What if it is?

HONEY: Boy, you don't get very excited about anything, do you? *(She lies back down next to the* YOUNG MAN *moving closer and trying to turn him on.)*

YOUNG MAN: Only when it counts.

HONEY: I'll bet you're really something when you get excited. How come you don't get a haircut?

YOUNG MAN: 'Cause my pappy told me that one day I'd make my living from my hair.

HONEY: Are you making fun of me?

YOUNG MAN: No. It's true. My Pappy was way ahead of his time. He said, son, in a few years all a young man'll have to do to make a few bucks is just grow his hair long and set on a street corner and things'll just start happening to him. Like magic.

HONEY: Do you believe in magic?

YOUNG MAN: I used to. I walked through the crowd. I saw my best friends there. Real friends. I felt such a warm bond between us. Like we were all in the same place at the same time for the same reason.

HONEY: What are you talking about?

YOUNG MAN: And suddenly I felt free, my mind was lifting up, up, up in flight. Not like that thirteen year old wild, crazy, out of the house on Friday night feeling but something much deeper. Like nothing could hurt me. Nothing could touch my peace.

HONEY: Boy, you're really weird.

YOUNG MAN: It was like all that oppression from the month before had suddenly cracked open and left me in space. The election oppression: Nixon, Wallace, Humphrey. The headline oppression every morning with one of their names on it. The radio news broadcast, TV oppression. And every other advertisement with their names and faces and voices and haircuts and suits and collars and ties and lies. And I was all set to watch "Mission: Impossible" when Humphrey's flabby face shows up for another hour's alienation session. Oh please say something kind to us, something soft, something human, something different, something real, something—so we can believe again. His squirmy little voice answers me, "You can't always have everything your way." And the oppression of my fellow students becoming depressed. Depressed. Despaired. Running out of gas. "We're not going to win. There's nothing we can do to win." This is how it begins, I see. We become so depressed we don't fight anymore. We're only losing a little, we say. It could be so much worse. The soldiers are dying, the Blacks are dying, the children are dying. It could be so much worse. Everything must be considered in light of the political situation. No getting around it. It could be so much worse.

HONEY: Think about something nice.

YOUNG MAN: Let's wait till four years from now when we can take over the Democratic Party. Teddy Kennedy is still alive. Let's not do anything at all. It can only get worse. Let's give up. And then I walked through the crowd of smiling people. They were loving and happy, alive and free. You can't win all the time. You can't always have everything your own way. You'll be arrested. You'll be arrested, accosted, molested, tested and re-tested. You'll be beaten, you'll be jailed, you'll be thrown out of school. You'll be spanked, you'll be whipped and chained. But I am whipped. I am chained. I am prisoner to all your oppression. I am depressed, deranged, decapitated, dehumanized, defoliated, demented and damned! I can't get out. You can get out. You can smile and laugh and kiss and cry. I am! I am! I am! I am! I am! I am! I am! I am! I am! I am! I am! Tonight. In this desert. In this space. I am.

(*Another flash of blue light that seems more prolonged this time. Again the beam of light goes across the sky from stage left to stage right. At the same time the body of the sidewinder lights up green and jumps. The rattle rattles and the end of the tail begins to twitch.* HONEY *screams and cuddles close to the* YOUNG MAN *who sits up slightly.*)

YOUNG MAN: What's the matter now?

HONEY: That snake! It's still alive! It moved!

YOUNG MAN: Bullshit.

HONEY: It did! It lit up green and moved. There! Look at it! It twitched! Didn't you see it!

YOUNG MAN: You're just hallucinating. Relax.

HONEY: I swear it moved. Listen! Can't you hear it? It's rattling. It's still alive! Sit up and look at it!

(*The* YOUNG MAN *lies on his back and stares at the sky. The sidewinder moves again. As* HONEY *watches it and talks, the sidewinder body slowly inches its way across the stage.*)

HONEY: Well I don't want to get strangled again. Once is enough. It's moving again! Hey! Hey!

YOUNG MAN: Take it easy. It's all in your mind.

HONEY: It is not in my mind! It's right there! It's moving and rattling and I'm looking right at it! Why don't you look and see for yourself. Please look at it. You're scaring me. I know I'm not going crazy! Who are you anyway! Hey! Talk to me. I've told you everything about me and you haven't told me one thing. Hey!

(*The* YOUNG MAN *suddenly grabs her and pulls her to the ground then rolls over on top of her. He kisses her and feels her up.* HONEY *screams and squirms. Another flash of light from above. The beam of light across the sky. The sidewinder lights up red and twitches wildly. The rattle grows louder as it inches its way across the stage.*)

HONEY: What are you doing! Let go of me! Let me go! Stop! Stop it! Get off! Get off of me! My husband's going to get you for this! Dukie! Help! Help! Somebody!

(*The* YOUNG MAN *rips off her blouse and starts kissing her tits and stomach.* HONEY *gets turned on and runs her fingers through his hair.*)

Oh. Oh. OOOOOOOOH. Yes. Yes. Oh. Lick me. Lick me. Yes. Oh. You're fantastic. Oh. Yes. Yes. Yes. Lick me! Lick me!

(*The* YOUNG MAN *stops suddenly and stands up, straddling* HONEY *with his legs.*)

What's the matter? You can kiss me. It's all right. What's wrong? You're really weird, mister. I'm leaving. I want to leave!

(*The* YOUNG MAN *looks up at the sky with his back to the*

audience and stares. HONEY *begins to panic. From this point on there are more frequent blasts of blue light. Each time the sidewinder lights up alternately green and red and the rattling grows louder as he slithers and inches across the stage.)*

YOUNG MAN: It's all going to happen now.

HONEY: What is? I'm leaving here !

(She tries to leave. The YOUNG MAN *puts his foot gently on her chest and pushes her back down.)*

YOUNG MAN: You can't. We're caught. We're captured.

HONEY: Not me! Nobody's capturing me or kidnapping me or anything else! I'm free! I can come and go anywhere I like! You can't make me stay here!

YOUNG MAN: You're right.

(He lets her up. She stands but can't move. She seems almost hypnotized.)

HONEY: Wait a minute. Wait ... What did you give me anyway? What was in that needle? You're no diabetic! I've seen diabetics before and you're not one of them! Who are you anyway? How did you get here? Where are you from?

YOUNG MAN: I am from the planet Crypton. No. I am from the Hollywood Hills. No. I am from Freak City. That's where I was raised anyway. A small town. A town like any other town. A town like Mama used to make with lace doilies and apple pie and incest and graft. No. It's not true. I am an American though. Despite what they say. In spite of the scandal. I am truly an American. I was made in America. Born, bred and raised. I have American blood. I dream American dreams. I fuck American girls. I devour the planet. I'm an earth eater. No. I'm a lover of peace. A peace maker. A flower child, burned by the times. Burned out. A speed freak. A Tootsie Roll, an Abazaba. I came to infect the continent. To spread my disease. To make my mark, to make myself known. To cut down the trees, to dig out the gold, to shoot down the deer, to capture the wind. But now I'm myself. Now I'm here. And it's all going to happen now. Right now. It's all going to happen.

*(*HONEY *collapses.)*

BLACKOUT

(Bright flash of light. Beams of light go back and forth across the sky. Then back to blackness. A sonic boom. Above the proscenium a large neon "Intermission" sign in red blinks on and off continuously as the song "Alien Song" by the HOLY MODAL ROUNDERS *comes on.)*

ALIEN SONG

You don't have to do me no favors
You don't have to tell me no lies
Just tell me what happened to my neighbors
When all I can see is black flies

It wasn't so long that I wandered
It wasn't so long I was gone
But now I come back and there's no wooden shack
And the turnips I grew are all gone

You don't look to me like a native
The way that you move is so strange
I wish I was feeling creative
But maybe it's time for a change

Maybe I took the wrong highway
Maybe I made a mistake
But this is the creek where I caught pollywogs
And I know 'cause I just took a drink

Maybe we could make conversation
I see that your lips have no skin
There must be a simple explanation
But how come you're wearing a grin

I couldn't go back where I came from
'Cause that would just bring me back here

And this is the place I was born, bred and raised
And it doesn't seem like I was ever here

It looks like your forehead's on fire
But maybe I'm losing my grip
It sounds like your voice is a choir
And now both my feet seem to slip

Now I can see my whole body
Stranded way down by the creek
It looks so alone while it looks for its home
And it doesn't hear me while I shriek

by SAM SHEPARD
Music by HOLY MODAL ROUNDERS

ACT TWO

Black stage. The houselights go down. The sun glows on stage and becomes brighter and brighter revealing the '57 Chevy seen in Act One, center stage. The three Blacks are seated inside. They are on the desert. The radio in the car is blaring Booker T. and the M.G.'s "Green Onions." The Blacks sit motionless and listen to the tune for a full sixty seconds. Then BLOOD turns the radio off with a sharp snap. DUDE and BLADE slowly open their doors on either side and get out of the car. They slam the doors shut and walk to the back of the car as BLOOD sits motionless behind the wheel staring straight ahead.

DUDE: Keys, Blood!

(BLOOD takes the keys out of the ignition and without looking back, puts his arm out the window and tosses them back to DUDE who catches them. DUDE unlocks the trunk and raises it. Inside are the YOUNG MAN and HONEY with their hands tied behind their backs and gags in their mouths. DUDE and BLADE lift them out of the trunk and pull them around to the downstage side of the car and slam them up against it. The YOUNG MAN and HONEY make muffled screams and protests as DUDE and BLADE pull out guns and level them at their heads, as though to execute the two of them.)

BLOOD: Hold it!

(BLOOD opens his door and slides out. He walks up to HONEY and the YOUNG MAN and stares at them, then reaches up simultaneously with both hands and grabs their gags and yanks them out of their mouths.)

YOUNG MAN: Hey Blood, what's....

BLOOD: Shut up!

HONEY: You guys better not hurt us. They got Forest Rangers out here. They make the round every half hour.

YOUNG MAN: What's going on, Blood? Did something go wrong?

BLOOD: Yeah, something went wrong. Your friend Mickey Free didn't make the drop.

YOUNG MAN: What? Why not? What happened?

BLOOD: You tell me.

YOUNG MAN: I left him with the dope. I trusted him completely.

BLOOD: Seems as though he took off into the desert with a very valuable computer and just forgot all about our plan.

YOUNG MAN: I don't know anything about a computer.

BLOOD: It also seems like there's a couple dead men in a garage somewhere who can easily be traced to a Volkswagen which can be easily traced to us.

YOUNG MAN: I had to shoot them. They were slowing me down.

HONEY: You shot somebody? You never told me you shot anybody.

YOUNG MAN: Shut up!

BLOOD: One thing I figured sure was that we could shape a psychedelic head any which way once we gave it the proper injections. Once we set it straight on a few political scores. 'Course there might be such a thing as an overdose of that technique. I mean I can dig it. The revolution looks old fashioned once you seen the universe. Ain't I right now. I mean all them lovelies floatin' around the street lookin' for a taste of acid pants and some insights into their karma and the right sign to match up to theirs. I mean there ain't much of a choice between balling all day and getting high or becoming a responsible revolutionary. Now ain't that the truth. I mean shoot, you didn't spend all them years fightin' the draft just to get the same bullshit from a bunch of crazy Blackmen.

YOUNG MAN: O.K. man, look.

BLOOD: Oh, now he's calling me man! He's speakin' my language! Yeah, brother! Bring on the chitlins! You gonna have to be a whole lot hipper than hip to get out of this mess, chump.

YOUNG MAN: I'm trying to talk to you!

BLOOD: Rap!

YOUNG MAN: I ran into a jam at a garage. The car was doing weird things. So I went into this garage to get it checked out. I was there for a couple hours trying to get it fixed. Then this crazy guy comes running into the gas station saying his wife got bit by a huge snake or something.

HONEY: When was that? You never told me about that.

YOUNG MAN: Just shut up!

HONEY: That was me he was talking about.

YOUNG MAN: Shut up! So this guy comes running in and gets the mechanic all hung up in his thing. So I shot him. I shot them both.

HONEY: That was Dukie! That was my Dukie! You shot him! You shot my Dukie!

(HONEY *starts screaming and kicking at the* YOUNG MAN. BLOOD *gives a command and* BLADE *steps in and jams the gag back in* HONEY'*s mouth. She goes on sobbing and kicking.*)

BLOOD *(to young man):* You're real stupid. You know that?

YOUNG MAN: Come on, Blood. I did everything you told me.

BLOOD: But nothing worked! Nothing worked! You fucked up! Now we're right back where we started.

YOUNG MAN: I can find Mickey. I'll go look for him and find out what happened.

BLOOD: There's bigger stakes now.

YOUNG MAN: What do you mean?

BLOOD: The Sidewinder Computer. That snake you heard that guy screaming about?

YOUNG MAN: What about it?

BLOOD: We want that snake. We want it bad. You dig?

(*A* FOREST RANGER *enters from right. The Blacks are very cool.* HONEY *desperately tries to gesture to the* RANGER.)

RANGER: You folks having trouble?

BLOOD: Yeah. As a matter of fact we are. We've been trying to get to Ubehebe Crater for the past hour and a half now and we haven't been able to find it.

RANGER: Well you folks should have stopped in at the Ranger station before venturing off on your own. This desert's no place to play around in.

BLOOD: Yeah, we realized that but we just got so excited about seeing the sights that we couldn't wait.

RANGER: Things are especially dangerous now since there were two men killed not too far from here just last week. We still haven't found the killer.

BLOOD: Is that right. Well if we see anything we'll....

RANGER: Is the young lady all right?

BLOOD: Sure, she just got a little sun stroke.

RANGER: What's she got in her mouth?

BLOOD: A wet cloth. They say that's the best thing for a sun stroke.

RANGER: Well not stuffed in her mouth like that. She's liable to suffocate.

BLOOD: She'll be all right in a little while.

RANGER: Say, how come she's tied up like that? Now wait a minute. I'm no fool.

(BLOOD *pulls out a gun and levels it at the* RANGER.)

BLOOD: You're the biggest fool around baby. Now drop your gun. Go on!

(*There is a long pause as the* RANGER *considers what to do next. Suddenly he tries to draw his gun and* BLOOD *fires three shots into him. He falls dead.* HONEY *sobs through her gag.* BLOOD *points the gun at the* YOUNG MAN*'s head.*)

BLOOD: Now you got one last chance to redeem yourself Charlie. That extra sized snake that Mickey Free's got is something we need. We need it bad. Now I want you to find it and bring it back to us. The head and all. You dig? Now if you goof once more I suggest that you and your foxey lady here head for south of the border and start yourself a pot farm or something 'cause we're gonna be after your ass.

(BLOOD *turns the* YOUNG MAN *around and cuts his arms loose with a knife.*)

YOUNG MAN: I can travel better on my own. Can't you take her back with you?

BLOOD: She's gonna lead you to that snake boy. Now you cut her loose.

(BLOOD *hands the knife to the* YOUNG MAN.)

BLACKOUT

(*"Bad Karma" is played.*)

BAD KARMA

I got that bad karma baby
Gonna lay it on you
Got that bad karma baby
Nothing better to do
And when that bad karma hits you
Gonna holler and moan
Got that bad karma baby
Gonna bring it all home
I try so hard
I try to behave
But that bad karma baby gonna lead me to my grave.

I'm as down as a wart hog on a summer day
I'm as down as a depth charge in my own sweet way
I'm a down bringing back biting evil thing doer
I was born in an outhouse and I live in a sewer
I try so hard
I try to behave
But that bad karma baby gonna lead me to my grave.

When I'm reincarnated I get meaner yet
You may think I'm the lowest it's a damn good bet
But if I ain't the lowest I'll find out who is
And if his karma's badder I will rip off his
I try so hard
I try to behave
But that bad karma baby gonna lead me to my grave.

by STAMPFEL & ANTONIA
Music by HOLY MODAL ROUNDERS

SCENE TWO

The song fades out. Candles are lit on stage. Soft yellow light comes up revealing a small cave in the mountains. The home of the SPIDER LADY. *She is a wizened old Indian shaman with long white hair, Mexican blankets hung around her shoulders and across her lap, long tooth and bone necklaces, turquoise rings, etc. She is seated cross-legged in the cave to stage left with several candles around her. Seated directly across from her is* MICKEY FREE *with the sidewinder's head held in his cupped hands and the red eyes blinking on and off and the tongue spitting out. Behind them, upstage in the cave are the two* INDIANS *seen with* MICKEY FREE *in Act One. They are also seated cross-legged and pass a small bowl of steaming liquid back and forth between them from which they drink. Around them are their rifles, ammunition and more candles. Hanging from the roof of the cave are several long ribbons, red fox tails and religious artifacts. Bowls of incense are lit and placed in niches in the wall of the cave with smoke gently rising out of them.*

MICKEY FREE: I am afraid, Spider Lady. I find myself holding a great power. I have not the wisdom to use it. Speak to me of its secret.

SPIDER LADY: A great war is about to begin. It will mark the end of the Fourth World and the preparation for the Emergence to the Fifth. Do not be afraid, Mickey Free. You have a part to play in this Emergence. Do not seek shelter. It is only materialistic people who seek to make shelters. Those who are at peace in their own hearts already are in the great shelter of life. There is no shelter for evil. Those who take no part in the making of world division are ready to resume life in another world. They are all one, brothers. The war will be a spiritual conflict with material things. Material matters will be destroyed by spiritual beings who will remain to create one world and one nation under one power, that of the Creator. The time is not far off. The head of this serpent spirit has come to you as a sign. You must see it through to its rightful end.

MICKEY FREE: What does it mean? This spirit head.

SPIDER LADY: In the beginning there were the Star Gods. They descended to earth in flaming discs and created two great clans of man. One, the Snake Clan, the other the Lizard. To each were given tasks. The Lizard Clan was to harvest the crops and raise the children and the Snake clan was to see to the spiritual needs of the people. For this purpose the Snake Clan was given a giant spirit snake to communicate with the Gods and keep peace in the hearts of the people. The Lizard Clan soon grew jealous and wanted the giant snake for its own. There came a day of the great tug of war between the two clans. The Lizard clan pulling the head, the Snake Clan pulling the tail. Suddenly the serpent spirit split in two parts, the head going with the Lizard Clan, the tail going with the Snake. At that moment it is said, the people lost all knowledge of their origin. The Gods vanished from the earth. The people were lost. The two tribes went separate ways and wandered endlessly and with no purpose. More and more people left the clans and wandered their separate ways, taking up homes and founding separate communities, until all over the earth there was mistrust and hatred. Then a vision occurred to a small group of chosen ones who today live on the high mesas of this desert. A blue star descended to earth in the form of a spirit from the Star Gods and told the people that their Emergence was at hand. It spoke of the severed halves of the ancient spirit snake and that they soon would be joined together again on a night of the great dance. That once the two halves were joined the people would be swept from the earth by a star, for they were to be saved from the destruction at hand. That soon after the spirit snake would again be pulled in half by the evil ones and the Fourth World would come to an end.

MICKEY FREE: What must I do?

SPIDER LADY: You must be strong. For too long now you have been used by the white man's cavalry, Mickey Free. You have cheated your red brothers to the south. You have tracked and hunted down your own kind for the white man's money....

MICKEY FREE: And for my freedom! Better to hunt and kill than to be trapped behind bars in their camp! How could I choose! Geronimo was ready to surrender! I had no choice!

SPIDER LADY: You must let this head speak to your heart, Mickey Free. You must see the truth of this myth I have told you. You can read it in the earth itself. In the stars. Within your own conscience. Take this powerful spirit and deliver it to those who await it. To the Chosen Ones atop the high mesa.

MICKEY FREE: But what of the body? I have lost the body.

SPIDER LADY: It will come. It is written. All things have a plan, Mickey Free.

(MICKEY FREE *bows his head slowly to the* SPIDER LADY *as the lights dim out.*)

(*"I Disremember Quite Well" is played.*)

I DISREMEMBER QUITE WELL

You'll pardon me if I act strange
but we've been out of touch
I know that time is on your side
but time can do so much.
Are you still making it with time?
I disremember quite well

Yes I can see as I come close
time has been good to you
Just for a moment's truth you almost
had the face I knew.
But now, of course, it's not for real
I disremember quite well

I used to know you when you turned
your water into wine.
You played the shell game with yourself
and won it every time.
But where are you going to keep your prize?
I disremember quite well

I used to walk on water too
and float above the sand.
And hang the stars like diamonds on my
outstretched greedy hands.
But I've forgotten how that game goes
I disremember quite well

And did you ever do whatever thing
it is you're for?
Or does an old idea like that have meaning
anymore?
The maybe that I loved has gone, but where?
I disremember quite well

by ANTONIA
Music by HOLY MODAL ROUNDERS

SCENE THREE

The song fades out. A woman STENOGRAPHER'S VOICE *is heard in the dark.*

STENOGRAPHER'S VOICE: Ready, Captain Bovine!

CAPTAIN BOVINE'S VOICE: All right. Let's see 'em.

(A large color slide is shown on the upstage wall in the darkness. All the slides are of outlaws from the 1800's. CAPTAIN BOVINE *speaks in the dark. The slides keep changing.)*

CAPTAIN BOVINE'S VOICE: Now these faces that you're gonna see here, Billy, are all known criminals that, as yet, we haven't been able to pin down. Besides the young man in question here, if you happen to run across any other faces that you might have seen on the desert, it would be more than helpful if you pointed them out.

BILLY'S VOICE: Nope. Not a one.

BOVINE'S VOICE: Well, take your time now. We got a whole stack to go through.

*(The faces keep flashing on the wall upstage. They get faster
and faster as they go on, creating a strobe effect.)*
Any identifying marks that you can remember? I mean
besides the long hair and bare feet. That's pretty common
amongst your outlaws anyhow. Any scars or things like that?
BILLY'S VOICE: Nope. Nary a one.
BOVINE'S VOICE: Did he have an accent? A limp? Anything at all
would be helpful, Billy.
BILLY'S VOICE: Nope. Healthy as a yearling colt, that one.
BOVINE'S VOICE: What about the others? Any of the others ring a
bell?
BILLY'S VOICE: Nope. Nary a one.
(The last slide is a full head shot of the YOUNG MAN *with a
moustache. It stops still.)*
BOVINE'S VOICE: Shall we go through 'em once more for you, Billy?
You might have missed a couple and it's very important for
our records.
BILLY'S VOICE: I think not. I mean— I think—
BOVINE'S VOICE: Yes?
BILLY'S VOICE: You folks wouldn't have a hot cup a' java layin'
around the back room here, would ya'? Jest a little somethin'
to wet the old whistle.
DR. VECTOR'S VOICE: Java? Java?
GENERAL'S VOICE: Lights please, Edith!
(The lights pop up revealing BILLY *with his pots and pans
sitting in a chair downstage with his back to the audience and
his pack on the floor beside him. Next to him is the*
STENOGRAPHER, *Edith, who is shutting off the projector and
turning the lights on, etc.* GENERAL BROWSER *and* COLONEL
WARNER *are sitting behind a table upstage, facing* BILLY.
CAPTAIN BOVINE, *Chief Inspector for the CIA, paces around
the middle of the stage, chain smoking cigarettes and dressed
in a gray suit.* DOCTOR VECTOR *is also seated at the table with
the* COLONEL *and* GENERAL BROWSER.*)*
GENERAL: Edith, would you get Billy a cup of coffee, please. Do you
take cream and sugar, Billy?
BILLY: Nope. Black like midnight.
(The STENOGRAPHER *goes out and closes the door. The room is*

plastered with Air Force insignia, the flag, photographs of planes, the desert, slogans, etc., including: "To protect and to serve" in large letters. The three pistols that the YOUNG MAN *gave to* BILLY *are sitting on the desk in front of the* GENERAL. CAPTAIN BOVINE *walks up to them.)*

CAPTAIN BOVINE: Now, Billy, you're gonna have to understand something here right off the bat. Unless we come up with some evidence leading us to this kid you say you got these guns off of then we got no other choice than to assume that these weapons belong to you.

BILLY: Oh now don't go handin' me that malarkey, Captain Bovine. What the hell's a prospector out in the middle a' no man's land gonna do with three newfangled irons like them.

CAPTAIN BOVINE: Exactly. What is he going to do?

BILLY: Nothin'! He's gonna hand 'em over to Mickey Free like he said he was 'cause Danny paid him to. That's what. Nothin' else. Shucks, the way you fellas carry on here anyone'd think there's a plot goin' on to overturn the damn government.

CAPTAIN BOVINE: Danny? Did you say Danny? Was that the kid's name? Answer me, Billy! There's no point covering up for him. If we don't get him someone else will.

BILLY: Danny, Johnny, Jimmy! I don't know what his handle was. I never paid it no never mind. We just got to know each other so well we didn't need no names.

BOVINE: Now listen, Billy. You may not realize it, since you've been out of touch with society for some time, but this country's in trouble. Big trouble. Over the past few years there's been a breakdown of law and order and a complete disrespect for the things we've held sacred since our ancestors founded this country. This country needs you, Billy. It needs your help to help root out these subversive, underground creeps and wipe the slate clean once and for all. You don't realize the trouble they've been giving us. Every time there's a holiday or a bunch of people want to have a good time and just peacefully celebrate some national hero or something, there's always a bunch of these creeps hanging around making faces and giving the finger and shouting obscene things around and carrying cards and doing wild dances and what not. It's become worse than a disgrace, Billy. It's not even funny anymore. There was a time when the whole thing was a joke. But not anymore. Now they've got sympathizers, inside agitators and con-men in the White House. All over the country it's going on. I saw it all coming a long time ago. Ever since those bushy haired creeps started infiltrating from England in 1964. Before that even. Playing Negro music and gyrating their bodies and stuff like that. I'm telling you, Billy, it's about time we brought this whole thing to an end. If we don't do something soon we'll be overrun with these creepy faggots and leather jacket types. Things have stayed the same for too long now. It's time for a change!

(The STENOGRAPHER *enters with the coffee and gives it to* BILLY. *Then she sits down behind a steno machine and starts taking down the proceedings as though it were a court trial.)*

STENOGRAPHER: Here you are, Billy. A nice hot cup of java.

DR. VECTOR: Java?

BILLY: Well now. That's fine. Thank ya', peaches.

STENOGRAPHER: You're welcome.

GENERAL: Captain Bovine, perhaps we could find out something more about this Mickey Free.

CAPTAIN BOVINE: Later. First I want to nail this kid. He's the source. Mickey Free was obviously a go between, just like Billy here. How does that make you feel, Billy? To know that you were used by this punk.

BILLY: No different. I knew it all along. Me and him was pals. I coulda' cared less about what his real aims were. We just struck it off real fine and let me tell ya', that's a rarity on the desert. Yessir. Why I could tell you stories—

CAPTAIN BOVINE: Good. Tell us a story right now, Billy. The story of how you met this kid and everything you can remember about him. We'll listen.

BILLY: Well I was out near the Harmony Borax Works out there trying to tap a vein that I'd had me an eye on for quite a spell. Seems like forever. Well, with me ya' know, it's more of a way a' life than anything else. I mean not like them weekenders what come out fer a taste a yeller fever, all hog tied with them electric Geiger counters and metallic metal finders and what all. Us old timers, a lot of us, don't really hanker for no heavy pay loads. Naw. Just a little chicken scratch to keep the vittles comin' is cause enough to keep us on.

CAPTAIN BOVINE: What about this kid?

BILLY: I'm a gettin' there, mister. And don't get yer hackles up on this old buzzard, sonny, 'cause I'm as likely to clam up on ya' as spew on about somethin' close to my heart when I ain't got no willin' ears to catch it.

CAPTAIN BOVINE: All right. I'm sorry.

BILLY: I come down off the shale part a' the slope and headed toward my burro when I look and see this here kid what appears to be takin' a sun bath. Yeah. Right out in the middle of the blazin' sun he's a lyin' on his backside and gazin' right into thet big yeller ball. So I walks up and right off I offer him some rashers and a hot cup a' java. Figured he could use somethin' in that belly. Looked like it ain't done nothin' but gurgle for the last fifty miles. So we set ourselves down and get right into talkin' and spinnin' yarns. And let me tell ya' he had some doozers.

CAPTAIN BOVINE: What did you talk about?

BILLY: Well, he told me some a' the galldarndest tales I ever did hear. Dope peddlers, prostitutes, pretty girls and I don't know what all. Told me one about some street up in Frisco where he stayed and had hisself a different woman every darn night for over a week. Now don't that beat all? Enough to make an old man skiddadle off the desert like a water bug.

CAPTAIN BOVINE: Did he ask you any questions?

BILLY: Danny? Never seen nobody with so many questions. Day in and day out he'd be askin' me stuff about the desert, the Indians, the sky, the night, the sun, the stars, any damn thing he could lay his brain on.

CAPTAIN BOVINE: How much time did he spend with you then?

BILLY: Must a' been well over a fortnight.

CAPTAIN BOVINE: How long is that? Let me see. A fortnight?

BILLY: Better part of a couple weeks. I thought you coppers was supposed to know everything.

CAPTAIN BOVINE: All right. It slipped my mind. You say he asked you about the Indians. What did he ask?

BILLY: Everything. Their magic, how they cooked corn. Where the reservations were. How to get to them. The different drugs and medicine. How to tell the tribes. The symbols, the legends, the religion. How to make water out of sand. Stuff like that. So after a while I figured if he was so all het up about the red man I might as well introduce him to a real live one. Let him learn from the horse's mouth. So I took him up to meet Mickey Free. He ain't a full blood but a half breed has all the wits of a Indian plus the gumption of a white man. Mickey's one a the few real wild ones left. I believe you boys might a' even heard tell of him. Seems like he helped ya' find yerselves some a' this Indian land yer settin' on right now.

GENERAL: Yes. The name rings a bell.

BILLY: Yup. Old Mick's been doin' dirty work for white men ever since he was knee high to a scorpion. Most Injuns hat his guts. Say he's cold-blooded, turns in his own kind. Yup. He's the one supposed to have out-foxed Geronimo. Boxed him into a canyon or somethin'.

COLONEL: Captain Bovine, do we have to sit here all day listening to this? There's important business at hand!

GENERAL: Please, Warner.

CAPTAIN BOVINE: Let me handle this, gentlemen. Now listen, Billy. You'll have to understand that what we're primarily interested in here is the young man who gave you these guns and how it's tied up with these Indian affairs. You can skip all the local color.

BILLY: Well I'll try to scrape it right down to the bone for you fellas, but there's an awful lot bouncin' around this old head a' mine. Can't rightly figure where one thing leaves off and the other begins.

CAPTAIN BOVINE: We understand. It would help if you could clear up the connection between Mickey Free and this punk for us.

BILLY: Well, like I say. I left Johnny off up there at Mickey's wikiup. They hit if off like grease hits the skillet, them two. Just a cracklin' back and forth between 'em. They stuck it out together for quite a spell, then that blond boy up and left. He come back to me and started talkin' all different from what he done before. Talkin' about a plan with a bunch a poor folk back in the city. How I was to figure in this play by deliverin' guns to Mickey. Then one night I'm sittin' out there in a lonely spot, moonlit and all, waitin' for Danny when I hears these low kind a' moanin' sounds and I looks down and layin' right in front a' me there is—

CAPTAIN BOVINE: Just the pertinent facts, Billy!

BILLY: Boy, I do believe you fellas wouldn't let the light a' day shine on a sidewinder in the zoo, 'less you had the keeper there beside ya'.

(DR. VECTOR *stands abruptly.*)

DR. VECTOR: Sidewinder! Did what you say was sidewinder?

GENERAL: Take it easy, Doc. Sit down.

COLONEL: He did say "sidewinder" though. I heard him say it.

CAPTAIN BOVINE: Why did you mention the word "sidewinder," Billy?

BILLY: Just came off the top of the head, gents. The Hopis say the top of the head has a door and if you keep that door open all kind a' wonders come to ya'.

CAPTAIN BOVINE: Have you ever heard that word used on the desert before?

BILLY: You must be pullin' my long johns, sonny. That's a snake. A tiny poisonous rattler what likes the shade and—

CAPTAIN BOVINE: Did you ever hear the kid use that word? Answer me!

BILLY: I think if it's all the same to you, boys, I'll just mosey on.

(BILLY *starts to get up.* CAPTAIN BOVINE *shoves him back down in his seat.* DR. VECTOR *sits back down.*)

CAPTAIN BOVINE: You'll stay right here until you're released. Withholding information from a government official is punishable by law, in case you're not aware of it.

BILLY: Well slap my daddy. Thought I was too old to get myself into more trouble.

CAPTAIN BOVINE: Whether you like it or not, Billy, you've gotten yourself mixed up in a pretty messy situation. A very confidential government authorized computer has escaped from this Air Force base. This computer goes under the code name of "Sidewinder." Your mention of the name has only further confirmed our suspicions that you are in some way connected with its disappearance. Unless you reveal to us more useful information in this regard then I will have no other recourse than to arrest you for possession of arms without a license.

BILLY: The only reason I was— It was just a figure o' speech. I mean— I was a' gettin' set to tell ya' about this other snake that I seen.

(DR. VECTOR *rises again. The* GENERAL *coaxes him back in his wheelchair.*)

DR. VECTOR: Snake! What snake?

BILLY: Like I say, I was waitin' for my rendezvous with Danny when I hears these groanin' sounds comin' out a' the night. I looks down and there in front of me I sees this pretty young thing all tangled up in the biggest most gigantic galldanged sidewinder I ever did see. I mean I think it was a sidewinder. It had them tell-tale horns over the eye sockets. But she was so damn big!

(DR. VECTOR *lets out a jubilant shout. He starts buzzing around in his wheelchair.*)

DR. VECTOR: That's it! My sidewinder! It's alive! My sidewinder is alive! It lives! It lives! My beautiful sidewinder lives! Beautiful, beautiful sidewinder!

GENERAL: Doctor, please! Dr. Vector! Calm yourself!

BILLY: Nope. It's dead.

(DR. VECTOR'*s wheelchair comes to a screeching halt.*)

DR. VECTOR: Dead!

BILLY: I mean I think so. It has to be.

DR. VECTOR: What does this mean! You just said it lived! It was alive!

COLONEL: What's this all about.

CAPTAIN BOVINE: Explain yourself, Billy.

BILLY: Well I seen the head up on top of the high mesa with Mickey. They were worshipping the damn thing. Minus the body. I went lookin' for Mickey up at his wikiup but he'd flew the coop. Couple a' his side kicks says he went off to the high mesa to take part in some ritual of the tribes. So I followed his trail and sure enough there he was right in the middle a' the most high falootin' ceremony I ever did see. And I seen plenty. Lots a' tribes were there. All gathered together peaceable like and gathered around the snake head like it were some kind a' god or somethin'. And there was Mickey, old "one eye" himself, just a' sittin' there pretty as ya' please, beamin' from ear to ear and holdin' that head right in his lap. So I sallies over to him and show him the guns. Figured he'd be pleased as punch. But nothin' doin'. All of a sudden the whole shootin' match comes to a dead stop and they all just stand there a' starin' right at me like I brought the devil hisself. Well right off the bat I could tell I done somethin' out a' step. Then I look in Mickey's face and see that toothy grin a' his disappear fast as a swaller and he stands up and looks real serious and sad and mad all at once and tells me he don't want nothin' never more to do with guns or killin'. I mean I like to drop my silver fillin's right on the spot. Words like that comin' from the most feared Injun killin' bronco the West ever knowed. Then he reaches in his pouch and pulls out these here little plastic bags and tells me to take the guns and these bags back to the white devil what he got 'em from.

CAPTAIN BOVINE: What bags? What do you mean?

BILLY: Right here. I got 'em right in my pack.

(BILLY reaches into his pack and pulls out the plastic bags of dope that the YOUNG MAN had given MICKEY FREE in Act One. BOVINE snatches them away. Rips them open, wets his finger and sticks it in the bag, then tastes the powder. He marches to the telephone and picks it up.)

CAPTAIN BOVINE: Hello. Get me a special detail of Desert Tactical Troops over here immediately. It's an emergency!

(BOVINE hangs up the phone. BILLY stands.)

DR. VECTOR: But what of my sidewinder!

BILLY: You can't send no soldiers out there, Captain Bovine. They'll interfere with the ceremony. The Indians won't hanker to it one bit. You better pick up that phone and call off them troops. I ain't kiddin', Captain. That's serious business them red skins are up to. I wouldn't mess with it to save my soul.

CAPTAIN BOVINE: Pipe down, old timer. It's just a routine checkup.

BLACKOUT

("CIA Man" comes on in the dark.)

C.I.A. MAN

Who can tell if Egypt's got the bomb
Even if the atmosphere is calm

Fuckin A Man C.I.A. Man

Who can train guerillas by the dozen
Train 'em all to kill their untrained cousins

Fuckin A Man C.I.A. Man

Who can plant the bug on anyone
Who would never eavesdrop just for fun

Fuckin A Man C.I.A. Man

Who will do just what he has to do
All the way from Dallas to Peru

Fuckin A Man C.I.A. Man

Why is Mao scared to start a hassle
Mao isn't man enough to rassle

Fuckin A Man C.I.A. Man

Who is diplomatically immune
Who else but the hero of this tune

Fuckin A Man C.I.A. Man

by PETER STAMPEL, TULI KUPFERBURG & ANTONIA
Music by HOLY MODAL ROUNDERS
Copyright—United International 1966

SCENE FOUR

The song fades out. Total silence. Black stage. Thundering sound of many feet pounding on the floor. Silence. Low moaning sound of many voices chanting in unison.

HOPI CHANTS

The lights come up slowly as the chanting goes on. Center stage is MICKEY FREE's wikiup, a small oval shaped structure made out of bent twigs, old sheets of metal, mud, strips of cloth and a dark blanket covering the door. A thin column of smoke comes from the top. Stage left of the wikiup is a group of eight INDIANS seated in a semi-circle around an open pit. These are the SNAKE PRIESTS. They are chanting and preparing themselves for a ceremony. In front of them are three large pottery jars, the tops covered with antelope skins. Behind them is the snake altar: a large screen of antelope skin stretched on four long sticks. Three large Hopi Kachina dolls are painted on the skin with other symbols, semi-circles and figures. Large snake bodies and heads protrude from the skin in bright colors; these operate like hand puppets from behind the screen, so at a certain point in the ceremony they·will come alive and wriggle to the dance.

In front of the screen are several stalks of corn and tall poles with feather and ribbon streamers dangling from their tops. Encircling the entire group and the altar is a line of sacred yellow cornmeal. All the INDIANS are very dark skinned, have long black hair with eagle feathers at the back of the neck, are naked except for loin cloths and moccasins. A large white oval is painted over each of their breasts and shoulder blades, their foreheads and the fronts of their throats are painted white, the rest of their faces are painted black, the forearms and legs below the knees are painted *white. They each wear turquoise and shell necklaces; their loin cloths are blue with a black snake design in front and back. They wear belts with long fringe around the waist, and a fox skin and tail fastened to the belt in the rear. Tied to each right knee is a tortoise shell rattle. Their moccasins are reddish brown buckskin with fringe and shell designs. They wear white armlets around the bicep and anklets just above the moccasins. The* CHIEF SNAKE PRIEST, *who sits more or less in the center, holds a bow standard decorated with feathers and horsehair.*

They chant in a low moaning unison for a while and sway from side to side. The CHIEF SNAKE PRIEST *slowly places both his hands on one of the jars, the others follow and place their hands on the other two jars. The* CHIEF *removes the skin from the top of the jar and tips the jar toward the pit. The other priests do the same with their jars. The chanting mounts in volume and intensity.*

Suddenly, on cue from the CHIEF, *they all dip the jars down into the pit. Dozens of snakes of all sizes and colors slither from the jars into the pit. The chanting keeps up until all the snakes have disappeared into the pit.*

HONEY *and the* YOUNG MAN *pop onto the stage from left; the sidewinder's body is in the* YOUNG MAN'S *hand. The* INDIANS *are jolted into silence. The* YOUNG MAN *and* HONEY *stare at them. The* INDIANS *rise in unison and walk off left.*

HONEY: Maybe we oughta' come back tomorrow.

YOUNG MAN: Shut up.

HONEY: Look, I've done my bit already. I found you your dumb snake so why don't you let me go. You said before that I just slowed you down.

YOUNG MAN: I need you around.

HONEY: 'Cause you're scared. You've been scared right along and you thought I didn't know it. Right? You're scared shitless.

YOUNG MAN: Will you cool it!

HONEY: No, I won't cool it! I'm not one of your hippie sluts you can drag through the streets and any damn place you feel like going! Giving her clap and hepatitis and everything else.

YOUNG MAN: Look—

HONEY: No, you look! You killed my Dukie! I'll never forgive you for that. Just 'cause I go to bed with you doesn't mean I forgot.

YOUNG MAN: Just hang loose a little bit longer, all right? Please? I promise as soon as we're through getting this snake put back together we'll go into town and have a really neat time. O.K.?

HONEY: Can we go to the movies?

YOUNG MAN: Sure. Anything you want. We'll get us some hot apple pie and coffee at the truck stop and then we'll go to the movies.

HONEY: There's a new Elvis Presley movie on. Did you see it?

(The low sound of chanting comes from the wikiup. The YOUNG MAN *sneaks toward it with* HONEY *behind him.)*

YOUNG MAN: I saw *Jailhouse Rock.*

HONEY: No. This is a new one. He plays the part of this stock car driver who always wins, so he gets real rich. But he's such a good guy that he gives all his money away to his friends and people who are poor. You know, he buys them cars and refrigerators and stoves and TV's and all that kind of stuff. But then he gets in trouble—I mean all his friends like him and everything and he's real popular but he gets in trouble with the Internal Revenue Service because they say he didn't pay a lot of his taxes. So he tells them he wrote off all those gifts as tax deductible charities. But the Internal Revenue doesn't go for that and they say he has to go and take back all those things that he bought for all those people and give them to the government. So he goes and takes back a few things but what happens is that all his friends start hating him because they think he's an Indian giver and everything. So—

(Suddenly the two INDIANS *who were with* MICKEY FREE *in Act One jump out of the wikiup with knives and pin the* YOUNG MAN *and* HONEY *to the ground.* HONEY *screams.)*

YOUNG MAN: Wait a minute! Wait a minute! Paza! Paza! Tanta

muy bien amigo! Amigo! Tosa entra por Mickey Free! Nada mas! Mada mas! Para Mickey Free. Entiende? Sabe?

(MICKEY FREE *comes out of the wikiup slowly. His face is painted with white zigzags. He is stripped to the waist and wears an embroidered loin cloth and high buckskin moccasins and an Apache headband around his head. The huge knife still dangles down from his crotch. He crosses slowly to the* YOUNG MAN *who is still pinned to the ground. He smiles and releases the* INDIANS. *They back off.*)

YOUNG MAN: Mickey.

MICKEY: Kachada. Why have you come back?

YOUNG MAN: I have to talk to you.

MICKEY: I talk no more of guns and drugs. Of plans to conquer worlds. If you come to get back your guns I have already give them to Billy.

YOUNG MAN: No. The guns don't matter. It's the snake. The snake you found on Honey. What did you do with the head?

HONEY: Remember? You saved my life. You cut off its head.

YOUNG MAN: This is the body. You have the head.

(*The* YOUNG MAN *holds up the sidewinder's body to* MICKEY, *who stares at it, then smiles broadly and lets out a shrill scream. He hugs the* YOUNG MAN *and picks him up, dancing with him and laughing. The other* INDIANS *smile.*)

MICKEY: You are the Pahana! You have come! You have brought us our salvation!

(MICKEY *grabs the sidewinder's body and holds it over his head, dancing with it wildly. The other two* INDIANS *join in. The* YOUNG MAN *tries to grab the snake back.* HONEY *lies dazed on the floor.*)

YOUNG MAN: Wait a minute! Wait a minute! That's mine! That belongs to somebody else! Mickey! Cut it out! You can't have that snake! They'll kill me if I don't bring it back! Mickey! You've got to give it back! Give it back!

MICKEY: The Spider Lady has told me the truth. She said you would come. The body would join the head of its own will. And now it is here. The ceremony can begin!

YOUNG MAN: What ceremony? That's a machine, you creep! It's

not real. The Air Force cooked it up to trace flying saucers! The spades want it to trace the Air Force. I want it because it means my life if I don't get it back to them.

MICKEY: My brothers and I have followed many separate ways, sometimes killing each other. Tonight we shall all see the kingdom. Tonight the spirit snake shall become one again and with it shall join all its people. You and your bride might also come on this journey, Pahana.

HONEY: He's not my husband. He killed my husband.

YOUNG MAN: That's a machine. Mickey. A computer. Not a god.

MICKEY: You are free, Pahana. You have brought us to our emergence. It will take us to a place we will never come back from. You are welcome to enter and follow us there or stay here on this earth and follow your will. The stars will watch you as you go.

(MICKEY *turns and walks back into the wikiup with the sidewinder's body in his hand. The* INDIANS *follow him in.*)

YOUNG MAN: Let's go. Come on.

HONEY: Wait. What did he mean?

YOUNG MAN: Never mind. Let's get out of here.

(*The chanting comes again from the wikiup, low and then rising.*)

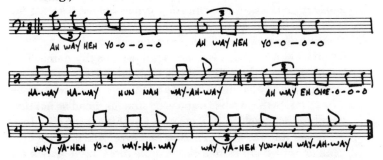

HONEY: What's that?

YOUNG MAN: Never mind! Are you coming or not?

HONEY: I never heard that before.

YOUNG MAN: They're sacred songs. It'd take you a year to understand the first word.

HONEY: It's so soothing. Like hearing the wind.

YOUNG MAN: I know. I know. If you get hooked on it we'll never get out of here. Now come on! Look, we gotta head for Mexico right now! Blood is going to be after my ass before too long. It was you who wanted to go see the movie before! Remember? Honey! Get up, and let's go.

(She is in a kind of trance state. She rises slowly and moves toward the wikiup. The YOUNG MAN runs to her and grabs her shoulders. He shakes her. She stares at him blankly.)

YOUNG MAN: Goddammit! I'm not walking back down into that desert alone! Do you hear me! It's the middle of the night! I might get shot for having long hair or smelling bad or something! Honey! Snap out of it! It's not for white people's ears! It's secret stuff! It'll make you crazy! If we go in there they'll never see us again! Never! We'll be scooped up! Taken away! Can't you understand me! I need you! I need you with me! I can't come back here again! Why don't you listen! Honey!

(He shakes her, then lets her go. She walks like a sleepwalker straight into the wikiup. The chanting reaches a kind of chord as she enters.)

Honey! You'll never see daylight again!

(A blue flash in the sky. The sound of a jet as the YOUNG MAN looks up at the sky. The chanting grows louder. The YOUNG MAN clenches his hands together and starts to say the Lord's Prayer as he walks slowly toward the wikiup.)

Our Father who art in Heaven. Hallowed be thy name. Thy kingdom come, thy will be done, on earth as it is in heaven. Give us this day our daily bread and forgive us our trespasses as we forgive those who trespass against us. Lead us not into temptation but deliver us from evil. For thine is the kingdom, the power and the glory. Forever and ever. Amen.

(The chanting grows to an incredible pitch as he enters the wikiup on the word "Amen." A pause as just the wikiup is seen with the chanting coming from it. Another flash of blue in the sky. Then the beam of light going across from stage left to stage right as in Act One. Then one at a time eight ANTELOPE PRIESTS come out of the wikiup in single file. They are dressed similarly to the SNAKE PRIESTS except they have painted

themselves ash gray with white zig-zag lines running up from
their breasts to their shoulders, and down the arms to the
fingers and down the front of the legs to their big toes. They
each carry a large gourd-like rattle and one holds a large
antelope drum which he pounds in a steady rhythm. Their
chins are outlined by a white line drawn from ear to ear. Their
loin cloths are white with black snake designs and embroidered
sashes. They are followed closely by the eight SNAKE PRIESTS.
They all continue the chant in a low murmur and walk single
file to the snake altar where they face each other in a double
line, eight on either side of the snake pit. Simultaneously they
stomp with their right feet on the floor. A loud boom like
thunder comes forth. They all begin to sway from left to right
in unison and shake the rattles in time. They form a circle,
then fan out into single file again and circle the entire stage
four times chanting over and over again in rhythmic pattern
and stomping their right feet in unison on the beginning
accent of the word. Each time they stomp, the sound should

come like thunder. The rhythm is slow, deliberate and powerful. Everything about the dance is spiritual and sincere and should not be cartooned or choreographed beyond the unison of the rhythmic patterns. After they have circled the stage four times they again go to the snake pit and line up across from each other, but closer to each other this time and forming a circle of bodies. They link arms and bend over the pit. They make a chord with their voices, rising from a low pitch to extremely high and shrieking. As they do this, the CHIEF PRIEST of the snake group kneels down and puts his head into the pit. He comes up with a snake in his mouth. The others fan back and the CHIEF SNAKE PRIEST dances with the writhing snake in his mouth. The ANTELOPE PRIESTS fan off and dance to the right side of the stage and stand in a line, swaying from side to side and changing as they stomp their right feet. The SNAKE PRIESTS line up stage left and do the same. One of the SNAKE PRIESTS dances out from the line toward the CHIEF and waves two long eagle feathers over the snake's head as the CHIEF dances with it. The snake goes limp and the CHIEF lets it drop to the floor. A third SNAKE PRIEST dances out with a stick and waves it over the snake then bends down, picks it up with both hands, holds it aloft and dances over to the ANTELOPE PRIESTS. He hands it to one of the ANTELOPE PRIESTS at the end of the line. He takes and holds it, coaxing it with one hand as he continues to chant. The CHIEF walks back to behind the snake altar where he starts to operate one of the snake puppets in short jerky movements. Another SNAKE PRIEST puts his head into the pit and comes up with another snake between his teeth. The same process goes on as with the CHIEF until each ANTELOPE PRIEST in the line has a snake in his hand and each SNAKE PRIEST has danced with a snake and returned to behind the snake altar to operate one of the puppets. Once this is finished the ANTELOPE PRIESTS are all visible, dancing and chanting with the snakes. The SNAKE PRIESTS are all unseen behind the snake altar, and the snake puppets are moving vigorously around. MICKEY FREE comes out of the wikiup. He is dressed the same way, stripped to the waist, but he wears a blue kachina mask on his head. He holds the head of the sidewinder in his left hand, the body in the right. He holds them aloft. Behind him are HONEY, the YOUNG MAN, and the two INDIANS from before. HONEY's face is painted like the SNAKE PRIESTS' and the YOUNG MAN's like the ANTELOPES'. HONEY wears a long black dress, a blue loin cloth over it and a white and red cape. Her hair is loose, with eagle feathers attached at the back. Around her neck is a necklace of turquoise and shell. She holds an earthen jar out in front of her containing sacred oil. The YOUNG MAN has an eagle feather tied to the front of his hair, his body is painted ash gray with white zigzag lines like the ANTELOPE PRIESTS' on his body, arms and legs. He also holds a jar filled with oil. The SNAKE PRIESTS come out from behind the altar single file and line up downstage. The ANTELOPES follow suit on the stage right side. One of MICKEY's INDIAN friends leads HONEY by the arm to the line of SNAKE PRIESTS where she kneels in front of the CHIEF. The YOUNG MAN is led to the ANTELOPES by the other INDIAN and he kneels to their CHIEF PRIEST. Both HONEY and the YOUNG MAN seem to be in a totally different frame of mind now. Calm, spiritual, totally accepting of the whole ritual. MICKEY stands downstage center, changing and holding the segmented sidewinder aloft, moving the two parts toward each other, then away. The SNAKE CHIEF and the ANTELOPE CHIEF exchange places and walk to opposite sides of the stage. The ANTELOPE CHIEF faces HONEY and the SNAKE CHIEF faces the YOUNG MAN. They each simultaneously place their hands on HONEY's and the YOUNG MAN's heads, then slowly push their heads down into the jars of oil they hold in front of them, so that their hair becomes saturated. They raise their heads up. HONEY and the YOUNG MAN stand. They are led by the respective CHIEFS downstage in front of MICKEY FREE. The CHIEF PRIESTS exchange positions again and then wash HONEY's and the YOUNG MAN's hair in the oil. They touch their heads together and then twist their hair together so that it becomes tied. The chanting continues the whole time. MICKEY, at the moment HONEY's and the YOUNG MAN's hair has been tied together, joins the sidewinder's body to its head. A tremendous bolt of blue light issues from the sidewinder, *matched by one in the sky. Thunder booms. The sky lights up blue again. The combination of the voices chanting reaches an incredible shrieking, like lightning. The whole scene crackles like high voltage wires. Then suddenly everything stops abruptly as three "*DESERT TACTICAL TROOPS*" with machine guns, pistols, helmets, uniforms, etc., enter briskly from right. The* INDIANS *freeze.)*

1ST DESERT TACTICAL TROOP: All right! Everybody put up your hands! Everyone! Put 'em up!

2ND DESERT TACTICAL TROOP: Let's see some identification! That goes for everybody! Get it out!

3RD DESERT TACTICAL TROOP: You people are in big trouble! You got any idea what you got in your hand there, buddy? That's government property! United States Government property, buster! Now let's have it!

(The 3rd DESERT TACTICAL TROOP *grabs for the sidewinder which* MICKEY *still holds over his head. A bright blue light comes from the sidewinder, then from the sky. The* D.T.T.'s *jump back. All the* INDIANS *and* HONEY *and the* YOUNG MAN *stay frozen.)*

3RD DESERT TACTICAL TROOP: Now look, buddy! I don't know what's going on here but that snake belongs to us! Now hand it over!

(The 3rd DESERT TACTICAL TROOP *makes another move toward the sidewinder and again it lights up, answered by a light in the sky.)*

You wanna get run in for resisting arrest too? We're not playing games here with you punks!

(Suddenly MICKEY *begins the chant "Wunti Hayano Diwitia" and all the* INDIANS *plus the* YOUNG MAN *and* HONEY *join in. They start to move slowly toward the three* DESERT TACTICAL TROOPS *with* MICKEY *leading them, still holding the sidewinder over his head. They begin to form a large circle around the* D.T.T.'s *as they try to get away from them.)*

2ND DESERT TACTICAL TROOP: All right! Hold it right there! Hold it!

1ST DESERT TACTICAL TROOP: Stop that singing! Stop where you are!

3RD DESERT TACTICAL TROOP: We're going to open fire in about

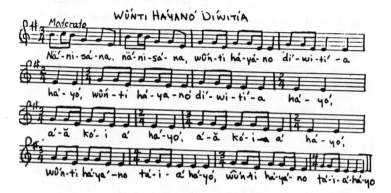

WŪŃTI HA'YANO' DĮWĮTĮA

Nä'-ni-sá'-na, nä'-ni-sá'-na, wŭñ-ti há-yá-no di'-wi-ti'-a

ha'-yo', wŭñ-ti há-ya-no di'-wi-ti'-a ha'-yo',

a'-ă ko'-i a' ha'-yo', a'-ă ko'-i-a a' ha'-yo',

wŭ'n-ti ha'ya'-no ta'-i-a' ha-yo', wŭ'n-ti há-ya'-no ta'-i-a'-ha-yo

three seconds if you don't stop and hand over that snake! One! We're not kidding around! Two! This is no joke! We mean business! This is your last chance! Stop in the name of the law! Three!

(*The* DESERT TACTICAL TROOPS *open fire on the* INDIANS *with their machine guns. The* INDIANS *keep coming. They form a circle with* MICKEY *at the head of it and the* DESERT TACTICAL *gain* TROOPS *in the center firing aand again. The* INDIANS *just sway back and forth to the rhythm of the chant. The sidewinder lights up, the sky lights up. The 3rd* DESERT TACTICAL TROOP *rushes straight toward* MICKEY FREE, *firing his machine gun into him.* MICKEY *just chants and sways. The 3rd* DESERT TACTICAL TROOP *reaches up and grabs the sidewinder and yanks it from* MICKEY's *hands. The body separates from the head again. Bright bolt of blue light from the sky. The* D.T.T.'s *scream as though being blinded. The lights go to black after the blue light, then back to bright blue. Each interval of light and dark lasts about five or six seconds. From pitch black to bright blue. Huge gusts of wind blow from upstage directly out into the audience, changing from hot to cold. Wind also blows across stage. Streams of smoke come from all around the proscenium arch and upstage. The chanting increases. A high frequency whine. The chanting becomes amplified. The bright blue light flashes on, the* INDIANS *are in ecstasy as they chant. The* D.T.T.'s *are cringing on their knees center stage. The lights go to black. The blue light again and this time all the* INDIANS *plus the* YOUNG MAN *and* HONEY *are gone. Just the* DESERT TACTICAL TROOPS *holding their ears and shielding their eyes. The lights stay up and become brighter. The whine and the chanting get louder, then everything goes black.)*

The End

OPERATION SIDEWINDER was first produced on March 12, 1970, at the Repertory Theater of Lincoln Center/Vivian Beaumont Theater, New York City, with the following cast in order of appearance:

DUKIE .... Robert Phalen
HONEY .... Barbara eda-Young
MECHANIC .... Michael Miller
YOUNG MAN .... Andy Robinson
FOREST RANGER .... Robert Riggs
BILLY .... Roberts Blossom
COLONEL WARNER .... Joseph Mascolo
CAPTAIN .... Robert Phalen
CADET................................ Gus Fleming
MICKEY FREE .... Don Plumley
1st COHORT TO MICKEY FREE .... Ralph Drischell
2nd COHORT TO MICKEY FREE .... Arthur Sellers
CARHOP .... Catherine Burns
BLOOD .... Garrett Morris
BLADE.............................. Paul Benjamin
DUDE............................... Charles Pegues
GENERAL BROWSER .... Paul Sparer
DOCTOR VECTOR .... Ray Fry
SPIDER LADY .... Michael Levin
EDITH .... Joan Pringle
CAPTAIN BOVINE....................... Philip Bosco
INDIANS .... José Barrera, Paul Benjamin, Gregory Borst, Gus Fleming, Robert Keesler, Michael Levin, Clark Luis, Richard Mason, Muriel Miguel, Louis Mofsie, Santos Morales, Garrett Morris, Jean-Daniel Noland, Joan Pringle, Barbara Spiegel
1st DESERT TACTICAL TROOP .... Robert Priggs
2nd DESERT TACTICAL TROOP .... Robert Phalen
3rd DESERT TACTICAL TROOP......... Michael Miller

Directed by Michael A. Schultz
Settings designed by Douglas W. Schmidt
Lighting designed by John Gleason